STRESS AND PEACE

Stanley V. Johnson MBA

WestBow
PRESS
A DIVISION OF THOMAS NELSON

WestBow Press books may be ordered through booksellers or by contacting:

WestBow Press
A Division of Thomas Nelson
1663 Liberty Drive
Bloomington, IN 47403
www.westbowpress.com
1-(866) 928-1240

ISBN: 978-1-4497-9467-5 (sc)
ISBN: 978-1-4497-9469-9 (hc)
ISBN: 978-1-4497-9468-2 (e)

Library of Congress Control Number: 2013908381

Printed in the United States of America.

WestBow Press rev. date: 06/18/2013

About the Author

Stanley V. Johnson was born in Mallappally in the state of Kerala, South India. In 1969, he immigrated to the United States. He was accompanied by his wife, Rachel, and daughter, Sheeba, who was born in 1966. Later, he and his wife had a son, Stuart Johnson, who was born in 1972 in Texas.

Mr. Johnson was a member of a minority group throughout his life and experienced the discrimination that accompanies this status. In India, he was a Christian, a minority religion. He spoke Malayalam as his primary language. He studied in Andhra state, where Telugu was the primary language. He then worked in Delhi, where they spoke Hindi.

Upon his arrival in America, he was once again a minority. He looked different and spoke with a distinct accent. Despite all of these differences, his ability to adapt to diverse situations enabled him to be very tolerant and nonjudgmental. He was very blessed with the ability to readily see other people's perspectives.

He earned a Master of Business Administration from the University of Dallas in 1975. He was the first member of his family to earn an MBA. During his career, he held various positions, such as accounting clerk, accountant, accounting manager, director of budget and planning, controller, vice president of finance, and chief financial officer and retired as general manager of Florida operations for a major transportation company. He enjoyed turning around financially troubled corporations and was recognized in *Who's Who in Business* in 1975.

He maintains a happy, peaceful life and likes to play cards, soccer, volleyball, tennis, golf, and other games. He is kind to other people and helps everyone he can. As a memorial to his parents, his family members established a scholarship fund in Kerala, India to empower the underprivileged with higher education. He currently lives in Florida with his wife, Patty, who is from Alabama. As a diverse couple, they enjoy God, church, family, and friends.

His daughter, Sheeba, is married to Robert Lee, Jr. He is of Chinese-Irish descent. Together, Bob and Sheeba operate one of the largest martial arts schools in Maryland. They currently hold sixth- and fifth-degree black belts, respectively. They have four children—Robert, Madeline, Alexis, and Grant.

His son, Stuart, graduated from the University of California and earned his JD from Loyola Law School in 1997. He is married to Julie, who is of Jewish Russian descent. Stuart is currently a partner with the law firm, Carico, Johnson, and Toomey, LLP at El Segundo, California. He was the Republican Nominee for 36th district for US Congress in 2002. He is a born again Christian and an Iron Man. Stuart and Julie, have two children, Hatcher and Madeline.

This book is dedicated to his wife, Patty; daughter, Sheeba Lee; and son, Stuart Johnson, and their families. The encouragement and support of his wife and children were instrumental in the writing of this book.

The author's reasons for writing this book are his inspiration, belief, business background, and observations of and associations with many people facing stress and lack of peace. He is a person with very little stress and an abundance of peace.

He is very grateful to Mr. Terry Devaney, MS, Purdue University, and consultant for World Bank; Major Chuck Bradley, MA of Social Security Administration; Susan Bradley, MS of Florida Deaf-Blind Association; Mrs. Leila Philip, MA, MEd from Canada; and many other people who helped in reviewing and giving constructive ideas.

Mr. Johnson thanks God for enabling him to write this book. He hopes that this will help readers trade stress for peace.

Table of Contents

Introduction

The purpose of this book is to discuss various stresses we face in our lives and how we can find peace despite of all these stresses. We face many stresses throughout our lives, beginning from very early childhood, as adolescents, as employees, as spouses, and until we die. Most everyone during his or her life faces some short-term or long-term stress. How we handle stress depends on each individual. Some people can handle it very well, and others cannot.

This book is written from my experience, social involvements, challenging job experiences, faith, and inspiration to assist people who live in stress. This is guidance for all, especially those in the younger generation who have many years left to manage their talent and resources properly and live in hope, belief, and peace. This is also good tool for growing families, retired and elderly people.

My experience growing up as the seventh of ten children helped me to understand the stresses my parents faced raising us with their limited resources. My father was a teacher and my mother a homemaker. They gave us their love and spent a lot of quality time with us. We did not have many material things but had a wonderful family relationship that served me well in my life. This lifestyle helped us to face stress properly and live more at peace.

My experience in my career, international travels, prison ministry work, management consulting, and many other associations made me realize that all people go through a lot of stress. It prompted me to research further and I observed various stressful situations. My inspiration and God's guidance helped me to find out how to obtain peace despite of all these stresses.

We will all go through each phase of our lives, try to understand different stresses, and find out how we can handle our stress and make our lives more peaceful. Sometimes the stress is for improvement; most of the time, it affects us adversely. The intent of this book is to assist you in evaluating your particular stress situation and help you find a solution through various recommendations.

When we believe in God and follow His discipline, life becomes easier, and we become content and happy. So our purpose in life is to establish God's discipline in ourselves, our families, the society we live in, and the universe. We must not lose faith and instill truth in our actions. Let us all try to live out our purposes righteously so that we can reduce our stress and live in peace.

I hope that this book will help you to reduce your stress and increase your peace.

The Purpose of Life

What is the significance of our lives and our existence? This is a tough question for most people, especially those who are nonbelievers. Different people have different views about the significance of life. Everyone thinks from his or her own perspective.

If you ask a child, he or she may answer that the purpose of life is to play and have fun. If you ask an old man, he may answer that the purpose of life is to prepare for a peaceful death. If you ask an alcoholic, he or she may answer that the purpose of life is to enjoy all the alcohol he can consume. An educated person may answer that the purpose of life is to create value or fame for himself or herself and to help others. Sensual people might answer the question by stating that life is for pleasure. Very poor people might answer the question by saying that the purpose of life is to make a livelihood. Very rich people might say that the purpose of life is to accumulate more wealth and provide for others' needs.

The people with hope, belief, and love think that life has a purpose beyond "eat, drink, and be merry." They believe that God created us with our talents, resources, and time to supplement other people's existence. All of our lives, we must complement other people's existence.

Before we were born, our spirits were in the Creator's custody. He put our spirits in physical bodies that were similar to His and created us in this world. Then God said, 'Let us make man in our image, in our likeness, and let him rule over the fish of the sea and the birds of the air, over the livestock, over the earth, and over all the creatures that move along the ground'" (Genesis 1:26 NIV).

God knew that we could not make progress unless He left us to make our own decisions. This is similar to us leaving our parents' homes to build better careers. When He created us, He promised that His Spirit is always with us. We do not travel alone in our journeys. He created us in this world to experience joy and pain in order to strengthen us. If we make right choices in our lives with Him at our side, these choices will lead to peace. When we make our own poor choices and do not include Him in our decision-making, we might experience unhappiness and stress.

The question of the significance of our lives has been the subject of much philosophical, scientific, and theological questioning throughout the existence of human beings. Our existence is for social ties, consciousness, ethics of good and evil, free will, and the pursuit of happiness. Our life also involves our understanding of God and life after death.

Plato defines meaning of life as "attaining the highest form of knowledge, from which all good and just things derives utility and value and be duty bound to pursue the good."

Epicurus, the Greek philosopher (341–270 BC), states that "the purpose of life is seeking modest pleasures, to attain tranquility and freedom from fear." (From Wikipedia the Free Encyclopedia)

We all like to have normal and peaceful lives. However, during our lifetimes, we all go through a lot of stress and lack of peace.

Sometimes we have to go through short-term stress in order to meet or achieve our goals to the best of our abilities and lead happy lives. It is very important that we use our God-given time, talents, and resources to the highest level. We must feel good and happy about our performances and accomplishments when we stress ourselves to the optimum level.

However, we will face many stresses as a result of numerous factors during our lives. Some of the stresses are due to our own decisions, and some stresses are due to factors beyond our control. When we go from normal lives to stressed lives for a long time, we can lose our happiness and accomplishments. We might sometimes lose control of our goals, priorities, and plans.

If we are passionate about something, we can work hard and put in long hours to accomplish our goals without feeling major stress. We feel less stressed if we have passion for what we do and enjoy doing it. It may be stressful for others to observe our work habits. In order to improve ourselves, we make many decisions that create many stresses for us from the day we are born until the day we die. Stress is not always bad, especially when the end result of our efforts accomplishes our plan.

We can be peaceful by making the right choices in our lives. We have been taught by our Savior how to obtain peace. We must accept and follow His teachings to be peaceful. We can obtain peace by practicing true love and being grateful for what we have.

> Love is patient and love is kind. It does not envy, it does not boast, it is not proud. It does not dishonor others, it is not self-seeking, it is not easily angered, and it keeps no record of wrongs. Love does not delight in evil but rejoices with the truth. It always protects, always trusts, always hopes, always perseveres and never fails. (1 Corinthians 1:13)

Major religions, such as Christianity, Hinduism, Buddhism, and Islam, are based on love and tolerance for one another. Followers of these religions also believe in not hurting others, caring for others, not discriminating, helping the needy, etc. These actions will give us a lot of peace.

In every religion, we are taught to do the right thing, make our lives joyful, and live in peace. Similar to Christianity, Islam also teaches us to serve the God who created us. Islam means *obedience to God*. Islam reminds us about having constant, daily communication with God. Muslims pray at least five times a day to be grateful to the Creator for what He provided for them. We must worship, love, and believe Him. This will result in accomplishing more peaceful lives.

God created the universe for human beings' needs and created human beings for Him. We must not be slaves to our own bad habits, such as money, sex, hate, jealousy, etc. This kind of human behavior will give us stress and unhappiness. We understand and see that the laws and constitutions of human beings do not work in the long run. We keep making amendments to the US Constitution in order to accommodate our current needs. However, God's commandments and laws will never change.

Rick Warren, in his book *The Purpose Driven Life,* explains that "God has created us to; worship Him, build and enjoy family fellowship, learn discipleship to become Christ like and serve God by doing mission work."

When we live in His path, our lifestyles will change for the better. We become more content and hopeful. We will start loving other people just like we love ourselves. We will stop judging other people. All these actions will result in our accomplishing peace and happiness in our lives. This will also reduce our stress levels.

What Is Stress?

Stress in humans results from interactions between people and their environment that are perceived as straining or exceeding their adaptive capacities and threatening their well-being. We can have good stress and bad stress. If we do not have any stress at any time, we may be bored or may not live up to our potentials. It is nice to have some stress to assure us that we are using our maximum potentials for the benefit of ourselves, our families, and others. Stress should be a powerful driving force, not an obstacle.

However, if we spend large portions of our lives in stress, it can create health and mental problems, which can make our behaviors even worse. We all experience different kinds of stress from different factors. Whenever we think that events may be stressful, it is possible for us to manage our stress by preparing well before the events occur. Three out of four people experience major stress, and two out of those four people experience serious stress. Twenty-five percent of all prescribed drugs are for stress-related disease. (New England Journal of Medicine)

Survival Stress

When we are afraid that someone or something may physically hurt us, our bodies will naturally respond with a burst of energy. This will help us to avoid danger and survive dangerous situations.

Internal Stress

Internal stress occurs when we are always stressed. There are things that we worry about over which we have no control. This happens when we have hurried lifestyles and get involved with stressful events we can't control or have no business in to begin with.

Environmental Stress

There are things around us that cause stress, such as noise, crowding, and pressure from work, family, etc. We must learn to manage these kinds of stress.

Fatigue and Stress from Being Overworked

This kind of stress is built over a long period of time due to long working hours, long-term challenging schooling, unpleasant family life, etc. This may be due to a lack of time management and inability to relax and spend time wisely.

Stress is the body's reaction to a change that requires a physical, mental, or emotional adjustment or response. Stress is the physical, mental, and emotional strain that we feel when hurried, under pressure, or as a result of worry or anxiety.

Stress is a condition or feeling experienced when a person perceives that demands exceed the personal and social resources the individual is able to mobilize. It can be defined as a state that results from a transaction between you and the things around you. Stress can be thought of as our reactions to events.

Stress is not always bad, especially when the end result is happy—for example, a wedding event, birth of child, promotion to a new job, etc. Stress is not necessarily something bad; it all depends on how we take it. Stress of exhilarating and creative successful work is beneficial while that of failure is humiliating and detrimental.

Stress can be caused either by outside sources beyond our control or by us when we accept responsibilities beyond our abilities or resources. Stress is an ignorant state. It believes that everything is an emergency.

Stress can make us feel frustrated, angry, nervous, and anxious. Stress can create health issues, such as rapid heart rate, muscular tension, clenching teeth, sweating palms, lack of focus, fatigue, lack of sleep, anxiety, chest pain, depression, stomach problems, diarrhea, dizziness, hypertension, etc.

Stress releases hormones and glucose and can cause adverse effects for people with diabetes. This can also reduce longevity. In extreme cases, it can result in isolation, cruelty, and violence to the extent of murders. Stress can create many addictions, such as overeating, smoking, drinking, alcohol use, drug use, depression, etc.

Stress was always present throughout the history of mankind. The Bible shows in Job's writings,

"Yet when I hoped for good, evil came: when I looked for light then darkness came. The churning inside me never stops: days of suffering confront me" (Job 30:26–27 NIV).

"Stress is nothing more than a socially acceptable form of mental illness" (Richard Carlson).[2]

"But if any one turns away from my reminder, his life will be dark and narrow one" (Koran 20:124).

Stress can be managed well when we start having faith in God and leave the control to Him. "Humble yourself, therefore under God's mighty hand, that He may lift you in due time. Cast all your anxiety on Him, because He cares for you" (1 Peter 5:6–7 NIV).

"Therefore, do not worry about tomorrow, for tomorrow will worry about itself. Each day has enough trouble of its own" (Mathew 6:34 NIV).

We must recognize when we feel stressed and start losing control of our actions. Major stress symptoms include feeling negative, worrying, irritability, feeling isolated, depression, chest pains, frequent colds, eating less or more, using alcohol, smoking, and drugs.

We can reduce stress by delegating more work to suitable people. When we are very busy, we must learn to say *no* if we cannot do certain tasks. We must exercise properly and eat nutritious food. We must take time to relax and do interesting things. We must practice breathing exercises, try to meditate, practice yoga, or get massages.

We must join support groups to discuss various stresses we face and find solutions from the group's experiences. All the above actions will help us to ease our stress. When we are very prudent and not excessive in our lifestyles, we can overcome adverse situations without major stress.

What Is Peace?

Peace can be defined as "freedom from trouble, feeling of tranquility, content, and cessation of hostilities, relaxation, good friendship and serenity." (World English Dictionary) The ultimate goals of all human beings are to live in peace and die in peace. We are all searching for peace in our lives. However, most people are not able to obtain real peace of mind. We can obtain peace only by our own acceptance that we do not have complete control of our lives. We must accept the fact that God the Creator has total control of our life journeys.

Inner peace is a state of mind that is mentally and spiritually at peace with enough knowledge and understanding to keep oneself strong in the face of discord or stress. Inner peace of mind, serenity, and calm enable us to be free from the effect of stress.

When we give up control without shedding our responsibilities, we can have more peace. If we can keep our bodies, minds, and spirits pure, we can obtain more peace. However, as imperfect human beings, we are not capable of handling many of our major issues ourselves. Since most of the problems are beyond our control, we must try to equip ourselves to face these problems and seek help when needed.

We need to obtain physical, mental, and spiritual peace. We will list some areas of lack of peace and stress we have and what corrective actions we can take. Again, we want to emphasize the fact that there are many external factors that we have no control over, such as wars, natural disasters, and corrupted social systems, which create a lot of stress.

In order to acquire peace, people in eastern cultures practice meditation, yoga, prayer, Tai Chi, and other peaceful exercises. Eastern religions such as Hinduism and Buddhism practice contentment and inner peace. Dr. Weiss's book *Meditation* states that "to achieve inner peace and tranquility in our life the inner beauty is very important."

Peace has been always of the highest value to humanity. Peace at any time is better than war and dissention. The best way to attain peace in the world is to teach families to be peaceful in their homes. We must settle all arguments and differences before we go to sleep every night. We must work and live together as families.

If our children can observe peaceful behavior of their parents, they can see that peace can be attained and maintained through the use of intelligence and proper behavior. Once they see the vision of peace, it can extend to family, society, and the nations in which they live.

When you find peace with yourself, you will become the kind of person who can live at peace with others. Gandhi said, "There is no way to peace, but peace is the only way."

All religions encourage peace, tolerance and abhor violence. Most conflicts come about because of wrong interpretations of religious views by some people in the religious groups.

Christians believe that peace can only come by the Word and love of God.

> The meek shall inherit the earth; and shall delight themselves in the abundance of peace. (Psalm 37:11 NIV)

The Lord is my helper: I will not be afraid. What can mere man do to me? (Hebrews 13:6 NIV)

Blessed are the peace makers for they shall be called sons of God. (Mathew 5:9 NIV)

Do not let your heart be troubled. Trust in God: trust also in me. (John 14:1 NIV)

Peace, I leave with you, my peace I give you. I do not give you as the world gives. Do not let your hearts be troubled, neither let them be afraid. (John 14:27 NIV)

For God is not a God of disorder, but of peace. (1 Corinthians 14:33 NIV)

"Salt is good, but if it loses its saltiness, how can you make it salty again? Have salt in yourselves, and be at peace with each other". (Mark 9:50 NIV)

Hinduism was in existence as early as 5500–2600 BC. The Hindus started practicing from the Vedas (holy book) during 1700–1100 BC. The basic principle of Hinduism is *ahimsa*, which means not killing or injuring anyone. In Hinduism, all individuals have to somehow reconcile their differences so that the stress of their differences can no longer take over their minds, bodies, and emotions, causing them to perform injurious acts. In Hinduism, the term *nirvana* implies freedom from stress that will lead to peace. Hinduism teaches that the world is one family. World peace is achieved through internal means by liberating ourselves from artificial boundaries that separate all of us.

Let your aims be common and your hearts be of one accord and all of you be of one mind, so you may live well together. (Veda X 195)[29]

> The high souled person who desires beauty, faultlessness of limbs, long life, understanding mental, and physical strength and memory should abstain from the act of injury. (Mahabharata XVIII 15:8)[25]

> The peace in the sky, in the mind, in the air, on earth, in waters, in plants, in forest trees, in all Gods, in Brahman, in all things, the peace in peace, may that peace come to me. (Veda X) [29]

Buddha (the son of a king) was disenchanted by intolerance and ill treatment of different people like the untouchables. The basis of his teaching is that, "Hatred is never appeased by hatred. Hatred is only appeased by love."

Buddhists believe in peace and no harm. Buddhism teaches that world peace can be achieved if we first establish peace within our minds. Buddhism proclaims, "Peace comes from within. Do not seek it without" (Buddha, Sources of Insight, Buddha Quotes).[22]

Islam states that faith is only one God, who is the greatest reason for humans to live together with peace and brotherhood.

Moslems always welcome others with *"Salamu alaykum,"* which means "Peace be unto you." "Make no mischief on earth we are only peacemakers" (Koran 2:11).

The Koran explains how Allah welcomes the people who seek peace. "When Allah desires to guide someone, He expands his breast to Islam" (Koran 6:125).

The Baha'i faith presented a world-embracing collective security arrangement between all nations as necessary for the establishment of a lasting peace.

Sikhism teaches that all beings that are created are His; He belongs to all. Sing the praise of one, the immaculate Lord.

Judaism teaches that at some future time, a Messiah will rise up to bring all Jews back to the land of Israel, followed by everlasting global peace and prosperity.

As we discussed earlier, we are all looking for peace. We may not always find peace because of our actions or uncontrollable external factors. It is easier to obtain peace when we are content, grateful, and live in strong faith. We are the ones who create inequity, and only we can correct that sinful violence. Nothing breeds hatred and violence more than inequity. We must treat everyone fairly. Violence of any kind toward any living creatures makes peace on earth impossible.

> Imagine all the people living life in peace; you may say I am a dreamer, but I am not the only one. I hope someday you will join us and the world will be as one. (John Lennon).[17]

> If we have no peace it is because we have forgotten that we belong to each other. (Mother Teresa).[11]

> If you want to experience peace, provide peace for another." (Dalai Lama) [22]

> Those who make peaceful resolution impossible will make violent revolution inevitable. (John F. Kennedy) [18]

> If you want to make peace with your enemy, you have to work with your enemy. Then he becomes your partner. (Nelson Mandela) [19]

> If we ask people free to choose anything, they will always choose peace. (Ronald Reagan) [20]

If they want peace, nations should avoid the pin-pricks that precede cannon shoots. (Napoleon Bonaparte, Brainy Quote). [21.]

We have only two choices: to peacefully coexist or destroy each other. Peace is not merely a distant goal that we seek, but means by which we arrive at that goal. (Dr. Martin Luther King Jr.) 3

It is helpful when we are spiritually more involved with people with good values and discipline. Spiritual people can cope better with pain and suffering. We must start reading motivational and spiritual books. We must be more humble and pray on a daily basis. These actions will help us to see that we are a part of some greater life than the present life. This will result in reduced stress and higher peace.

In addition to all the religions, we have many organizations promoting peace. The United Nations was founded in 1945 with the motto, "To facilitate cooperation in international law, international security, economic development, social progress, human rights and advancing world peace." The Norwegian Nobel Committee has been awarding the Nobel Peace Prize since 1901.

We have seen many important personalities with a wealth of talents and celebrity status commit suicide early in life due to drugs, alcohol, and other problems. We also see high divorce rates among celebrities. We do not understand why they go through these tragedies in spite of the fact that they can have any material possessions they want. Wealth, celebrity status, and materialistic life are enjoyable but do not make people joyful and peaceful. It appears that they were not happy or not content with their lifestyles or affluence and was not able to find peace.

We must be able to empathize with others and experience their suffering as our own. Being compassionate and kind is the only way to make peace on earth. World peace is an ideal of freedom, peace, and happiness between all nations and people. We may not be able to change the world, but we can change the way we think and live. If enough of us do this, we will change the world for better. Close relationships with God will always provide us with more inner peace.

Stress and Peace during Childhood

As children, we are all born in different countries to different parents. This is God's decision and not ours. Children are chosen by God to be born where they are born. Children are brought into this world with many purposes. God gives children freedom to choose and exercise proper judgment without destroying their minds, bodies, and spirits. He is always there for the children throughout their lives' journeys. It is the responsibility of the child to accept Him.

Sometimes children may wonder why they are born the way they are and where they are. They could have been born into poor, middle-class, or rich families. They could be rulers, dictators, or royalty or have different ethnic backgrounds. They could have been born in different countries to different parents. They do not have the answers to these questions, and it really does not matter. They must understand that the circumstances of their birth are God's choice and not theirs. We must accept where God places us.

The happiest moment in any parent's life is when a child is born. Children are loved, cared for, and protected by their parents. Parents, however, may have to stretch themselves to meet the child's needs, which can cause stress, despite the happiness they derive from their newborn children.

Children born to people with the fewest resources might have stress, because their parents cannot provide everything they need, such as proper clothes, food, and accommodations. Parents with the most resources might go through stress because they want to provide everything that is best for the newborn. They experience stress as they make enough time in their busy schedules. This means that even when parents feel the happiness of their loving newborn baby, they will go through stress.

Stress can result when a child is born unhealthy. According to the American College of Obstetrics and Gynecologists, each year, about 150,000 children are born with some form of birth defects. Three out of 100 children are born with major birth defects. Birth defects are the reason for 20 percent of infant deaths. Parents will endure a lot of stress to assure that their child is given proper medical care (Physicians Committee for Responsible Media, March of Dimes).

Parents have to go through a lot of stress, because they may not be equipped or capable of handling these problems. We have major stress because of the financial and physical inability of parents to support all the needs of sick children. It is essential that we all support these parents by taking care of the children so that the parents can have some time for themselves.

We must get parents all the support and resources available, such as providing financial donations and finding reasonable medical treatments and research. We must arrange to get free medical supplies from manufacturers, drug distributors, etc. These actions will help to reduce the financial and emotional stress for the parents. There are many charitable medical centers, religious medical services, and community hospitals that will provide free services to needy parents and children. We must always think that people suffering could be us. We must always understand that it is our duty to help others in need.

Childhood is considered to be the age from birth to eleven years old. In development psychology, childhood is divided into stages of toddler (when they walk and speak), early childhood (play age), middle childhood (school age), and late childhood. Toddler and early childhood stages usually include children as old as six years, middle childhood includes children from six to eight years, and late childhood includes children from age nine to eleven (University of Michigan Health Systems, Your Child Development and Behavior Results)

From childhood to death, parents are always concerned about their children's lives. When we were children, we depended completely on our parents. They took care of all our needs. So during childhood, it is essential that parents do not create an image of fear, terror, or control over children. Parents must give them unconditional love and respect and guide them properly. They must provide complete protection to their children.

Children must have enough freedom to discuss anything with their parents without any fear of repercussions. Parents learn about children by hearing their conversation, getting involved with their activities and trying to understand them better. Children must understand that parents are there to provide for their safety, support, and proper guidance. The purpose of building strong relationships with all these interactions with the children is to reduce stress and lead a peaceful family life.

When children are young, they may develop some bad habits, such as thumb sucking, head banging, head rolling, body rocking, teeth grinding, nose picking, etc. Parents must observe but ignore these symptoms, because most of these habits will be resolved by age or peer pressure. Parents must always assist their children by providing for their needs, praising them for good behaviors, and disciplining them for bad behaviors. If parents continuously push children and correct them all the time, the children will always feel stressed and suppress their mental developments.

Each child's development depends on many factors. The major factors are genetics for basic characteristics and the environment for physical and mental development. Parents do not know the exact extent of the role genetics and environment play in their children's development. For example, twins may look alike, but their characteristics may be totally different. In some cases, twins may not look alike physically but have similar characteristics. We cannot predict children's future characteristics with complete accuracy.

The development of the child is continuous, but age is not the only factor. When parents expect the children to grow up like other children, this expectation will create a lot of stress for children and parents. As discussed earlier, everyone is unique, and each person's genetic and natural development will be different. A person's development depends on his or her own uniqueness, and the final outcome will not be the same. Parents' understandings of these differences will produce less stress and more peace for children and parents.

A child's weight usually doubles in the first six months and triples in twelve months. A child's brain development is double that of an adult's between the ages of four to ten. Then the child's brain development slows until the age of sixteen, when it matches adult values. Children can learn languages and music faster at young ages than after sixteen years old.

The age between four and ten is the right age to teach children diverse subjects and activities. During these periods, they can absorb better than adults. It is essential that parents spend enough quality time with children and provide them enough guidance during their youth. They form their basic foundations of future development during these ages. Brain development, however, will continue forever as children learn and experiment with new things.

Some of this dependency changes during our childhood. Children start losing their pure hearts and innocent behaviors. Children sometimes criticize parents for not providing enough or giving more than they need and not teaching them the real values of life. Sometimes they have disagreements with parents. Sometimes children try to please their parents too much, resulting in not growing independently.

But as children grow, parents must understand that the children have to take responsibility for their actions in life. In addition to parents, there will be many people involved in molding their lives. They will interact with many good and bad people. Parents must insure that their friendships and associations are with good people. This will assist them to grow up as good children and build good character.

When children develop evil behaviors, they will face a lot of adversities. If they continue the evil behaviors, they can lose their self-control, which will result in very bad addictions, such as addiction to alcohol, drugs, immorality, and even crime. In the long run, evil behaviors will destroy them physically, mentally, and spiritually. This will result in problems with their education and create health problems. This kind of evil behavior will affect their entire development in their future. This will create a lot of stress for parents and children and the people they are associated with. It will adversely affect the peace of the family.

When children show their evil behavior, people will not appreciate it, and it can alienate them in their social activities and friendships, resulting in children's virtual isolation from those they love. These actions will result in stress and a lack of peace for parents, their peers, and other people they are closely associated with.

Hopefully, children will be encouraged and nourished by good habits and not attracted to evil behavior. When they face challenges and accomplishments as children, they must share those with their parents and grandparents. This will give them a feeling of a good support system and better accomplishments in the future.

Children must realize that their parents were once children, too, even though it may be hard to believe. Parents have learned many things from their own parents and understand the mistakes they made during their lifetimes. Parents try to protect children from the mistakes they make. Parents give guidance, advice, and punishments to the children for their benefit.

Again, these developments of children result as a combination of genetics and environmental functions. Characteristics also vary based on family, ethnic, and cultural considerations. They also depend on the health of the child. For example, a child with dyslexia can fail to attain the language, reading, and spelling skills commensurate with intellectual abilities. A child with an attention disorder cannot focus on things for a long time, especially items he or she is not interested in.

We may observe that the development of a child depends on his or her intelligence quotient (IQ) and willingness to participate. A child may be:

- Perfectly gifted (IQ of 180 and above)
- Exceptionally gifted (160–179)
- Highly gifted (145–159)
- Moderately gifted (130–144)

IQ is not a science, and these scores must be reviewed very carefully if a parent wishes to have a better understanding of the intelligence level of the child. Again, IQ will vary from child to child depending on the educational and cultural background of the family, available resources, environment and circumstances they live in. When children mature and behave well, there will be less stress for both parents and children. This will give a lot of peace to the family. Parents and children are equally responsible for accomplishing it.

Stress and Peace during Adolescence

Adolescence is a period when children get stronger physically than intellectually. In Latin, *adolscere* (American Heritage Dictionary) means "to grow up." This is a transitional stage of physical and psychological development between puberty and adulthood. This is an age when children start thinking abstractly, reason effectively, and are held more responsible for their actions. They try to separate themselves from parents and become more connected to peers. This is a period when parents or guardians allow children more independence. During these periods, they may question parental values. We must never lose sight of where adolescents came from and who they are.

These behavior patterns vary by country, culture, sex, family background, economic background, etc. During these periods, pressures from family, peers, school, social interfaces, and intimate relationships can create stress. These pressures are not always constructive for proper development for a child's body, mind, and soul.

This is a very vulnerable period and requires great care. Parents must see that children make the right choices. They must never take easy paths or shortcuts that could be destructive to their lifestyles.

Children must work hard to apply their talents properly and make their lives more constructive and productive. These actions are the strongest foundations for peaceful future. They must also realize that a few years of hard work and proper utilization of their talents and resources will help them to have better lives. Too many children take easy and irresponsible paths that will have negative consequences for the rest of their lives.

Children start attending schools to obtain educations that will serve them the rest of their lives. Children start learning new things in life, and they start gaining knowledge in different areas. The expectation of parents for their children to be always the best sometimes creates conflicts and stress for the children both physically and mentally. Adolescents and children must understand that these expectations by parents are for their own benefit in the grand scheme of life.

Adolescents must learn to acquire more knowledge and understanding from people they interface with on a day-to-day basis. They must become more knowledgeable, competitive, and inquisitive. It is essential that they follow righteous paths to have peaceful lives. They must try not criticizing and judging others based on their own backgrounds and perspectives, without knowing all the facts.

Children should understand that everyone is unique and created for his or her own unique purpose. They are never completely independent but are here to complement each other to accomplish the total purposes of their Creator. They must make good friends who complement them. Adolescents may not comprehend the total purpose of the lives the Creator had planned for them. They must always understand that they are part of His total plan. He always allows them to choose their directions, but He will never lose track of them. They will experience more peace in their lives by accepting His companionship.

"Christ is the end of the law, so that there may be righteousness for everyone who believes" (Romans 10:4 NIV).

Children are born and always develop as imperfect human beings. Sometimes they think they have total control of their lives. They feel that things like getting pregnant, sexual diseases and having accidents will never happen to them. They should never feel that all their knowledge and accomplishments are due to their own abilities.

Children must never forget the many people who guided and assisted them in their journeys of life. They must always be grateful to the people who helped them. They are given freedom to choose their lifestyles. They must make sure that all actions they take will strengthen them physically, mentally, and spiritually.

They must make sure that they exercise their freedoms wisely and properly to preserve their bodies, minds, and spirits. They must understand that excessive abuse of their bodies, minds, and spirits will create a lot of stress in their lives and the lives of other people closely associated with them. They must always consult with other qualified, educated, and experienced people to insure that their choices lead them in the right direction.

Adolescents must always take some time to cool down and understand and evaluate consequences of their decisions. When they are down, their likelihood of making wrong decisions is very high. During these times, it is always necessary to consult with people with more knowledge and experience. These actions will help them throughout their lifetimes. "Flee the evil desires of youth, and pursue the righteousness, faith, love and peace among those who call on the Lord out of a pure heart" (2 Timothy 2:22 NIV).

Consulting people with more knowledge and experience is just like consulting another surgeon prior to undergoing a major surgery. This will give them positive reassurance of the actions they plan to take. They should always make it a habit to consult others rather than depending entirely on their own perspectives. Two heads are always better than one.

It is essential for adolescents to be compassionate to others and love others the way they are. When they become adolescents, they may feel inadequate and stressed. Sometime they feel that others are better than them. Perhaps they believe that they are superior to others. All these self-imagined pressures are overcome by loving and accepting others the way they are. They must love and respect their caring parents, family members, and friends. If they do not have caring parents, supportive families and friends, they will grow up under more stress and feel depressed and inadequate.

In order to keep their lives stable, it is essential that adolescents seek good help and good company. This will enable them to have a better understanding of others and therefore have less stress in their lives. Excessive stress will cause them to feel inadequate and be unhappy. This can also lead them to develop bad habits, such as alcoholism, drug addiction, sexual addiction etc.

In order to have peace, they must understand from a very young age that they must love and respect their parents, families, friends, and others they come in contact with. They are respected by others because of their interactions with others, and they should show who they are and not what they have. Humility, kindness, love, care, and compassion are very important for character-building. Adolescents must learn how to command love and respect and not demand love and respect. They will realize at an early age that the more they demand, the less likely they will be able to accomplish their goals. They must never boast about themselves but rather praise other people for their special qualities and talents. They must always help the people in need and underprivileged.

Adolescents will learn that giving and helping others creates more happiness than taking. They will accomplish their goals and complete the overall plan of the Creator. The key to peace is to properly apply all their talents and resources given by their Creator to accomplish their plans and goals. In order to accomplish their plans and goals, they must stretch their abilities, which may cause some stress for a short time.

When adolescents develop a habit of giving, they will realize that they are fulfilling their life's purposes. They feel happier, at peace and can stretch beyond their normal limits. This will assist them in becoming more productive and put them in a position to help more to people in need. You never know if one day you may be on the receiving end.

However, stressing themselves for a long time beyond their abilities will affect their performances adversely with a resulting loss of interest. Stressing for a long time is also detrimental to their health and peace of mind. Adolescents must understand that proper growth is important for them, their parents, and other people associated with them. When they grow up to be accomplished people, their parents are proud of them. When they create these circumstances, everyone feels less stress and more peace. It must be the motto of children to be successful and peaceful.

Stress and Peace in Education

E ducation is the formal process of transmitting knowledge, skills, customs, and values from generation to generation. All parents want their children to have the best education and accomplish the best results for their futures. From the day children are born, their parents expect them to perform better than everyone else.

A competitive nature is driven into them; children are told to do the best they can all the time. It is very important to understand that parents do all this for the sake of the children's futures. If children ever feel that parents do this for their own personal benefit, children will end up resisting their parents. This can create conflict in families and end up in a loss of respect for one other. Under these circumstances, we all are under tremendous stress and without peace.

It is inevitable that parents and children will have arguments and disagreements that create stress and a lack of peace. If there is no respect in the family, children resort to bad habits, such as alcohol, drugs, sex, and other destructive activities. These actions will destroy them physically, mentally, and spiritually. This will further result in lot of stress and lack of peace in the family.

It is essential that children stretch themselves to the limit in applying their talents and resources to have the best educations and qualify themselves to perform to the best of their abilities physically, mentally, and spiritually. Growing up as an adult is the time when they must use every opportunity to seek advice from their parents and other experienced and qualified people.

Children must understand that they are solely responsible to acquire better educations and prepare for better lives, providing the best role models for generations to come. We must prepare ourselves to be the best, help parents by good performance, and obtain the highest recognitions and scholarships. A good education will help us accomplish our goals more easily, last forever, and help generations. This will make children's parents proud of them and at the same time reduce their financial and mental stress.

As previously mentioned, everyone has his or her own unique characteristics and talents. Children must never compare themselves with anyone else and not try to be like anyone else. They can learn good qualities from many people but can never be like them. In the event they try to be like someone else, they lose their way and create a lot of stress in their lives.

We all see people who are unhappy because they do not have enough material things. We must understand that no one can have all the material things he or she wants in his or her life. If material things are our major source of happiness, we will never be truly happy.

We see in our day-to-day lives that major movie stars, musicians, and industrialists resort to drugs, alcoholism, perverted sexual behavior, and even suicide. This demonstrates that joy and peace comes from within and never comes from our possessions. All the people mentioned above can acquire any material possessions they want.

We will be more peaceful when we start appreciating and being grateful for what we have. There are many people around us who have much less than what we have and still live in happiness and contentment. If we start understanding their lives and help them, we will be happier and will be at peace with ourselves.

We must make sure that we do not fail due to stress but always do the best we can. Failure to stretch and accomplish the most in life can make us feel that our lives are inadequate. We feel guilty when we realize we have not reached our full potentials. This will create lasting feelings of guilt later in life. Most of the time, we do not understand the complete purpose of our life journeys. It is God's plan and not ours.

We must use our God-given talents and resources to do our best—to create fullness in our lives. This will help us to accomplish what is best for us, our families, and others around us. We must realize that the talents given to us by the Creator are not only for us, but also to help others. The more we can accomplish in our lives, the more we can help and share with others in need.

We must enjoy our blessings but never indulge in excessiveness that will destroy our enjoyment in the future. Excessive consumption will usually result in financial stress and can create health problems. This will create a lot of unhappiness, stress, and a lack of peace in our families and with friends. We must worship God and not our possessions.

There is nothing wrong with having plenty of financial and other resources. When we give importance only for wealth, it is difficult to serve God. "For the love of money is root of all evil. Some people eager for money have wandered from the faith and pierced themselves with many grieve" (1 Timothy 6–10 NIV). "Jesus said to his disciples, 'I tell you the truth it is hard for a rich man to enter the kingdom of heaven. Again I tell you, it is easier for a camel to go through the eye of a needle than for a rich man to enter the kingdom of God'" (Matthew 19:23 NIV).

A rich person may have a hard time to believing the above gospel. The reason for the disbelief is that as a rich person, his priorities are for his own wealth rather than serving God. Again, Jesus said, "No servant can serve two masters. Either he will hate the one and love the other one, or he will be devoted to the one and despises the other. You cannot serve both God and Money" (Luke 16:13 NIV).

Our efforts and results should not be undertaken to compete with others but complement one another. We need to have students and teachers, musicians and audiences, doctors and patients, and other groups to make life complete. We experience good and bad situations during our lifetimes. These experiences make us stronger and more knowledgeable people and allow us to help others more. Sometimes, extreme adverse personal impact can strengthen us very much and prepare us to dedicate our life solely to help others.

There are many organizations formed by people who had traumatic personal experiences. Mothers against Drunk Driving (MADD) were formed to reduce drunken driving accidents. Jerry Lewis started the Muscular Dystrophy Association from his own personal experience. John Walsh started *America's Most Wanted* after he could not locate his lost son. His television shows helped us to solve many crimes of missing people.

A good education (knowledge) will enhance our ability to either build suitable career or start our own businesses. Our ultimate goal is to obtain careers in which we can contribute the most by applying our knowledge. We might go through periods of stress to accomplish our new goals.

We will see only a few people become very successful by their own intelligence, exceptional talent, inventions, etc. When we are young, we might feel that we can be one of them and live in a dream world without focusing on higher education. Only three out of ten thousand high school basketball players become NBA players, and only nine out of ten thousand high school football players become NFL players. (National Collegiate Athletic Association (NCAA) "Probability of Competing in Athletics beyond the High School Interscholastic Level")

Since there is a very small chance of any one of us becoming an inventor or professional athlete, our focus must be on education and making ourselves unique to accomplish our life goals. We must develop well-rounded careers, studying well as well as participating in games and sports. Most of the jobs that involve more physical activities last for a shorter period. Other jobs in which we use our intelligence last for a longer period. These are professional jobs—doctors, lawyers, engineers, accountants, technical experts, etc. We must educate ourselves well while simultaneously enjoying sports and games. We must always try to do the best we can and never take the easy way out. This will reduce our stress and assist us in living peaceful lives.

Stress and Peace in Employment and Entrepreneurship

Employment is defined as a relationship between an employer and an individual, with or without a contract. An employee's job performance is compensated by an employer in cash and/or ownership participation. As a rule, better-educated individuals get better-paying and more gratifying jobs (Hanford, Emily, Georgetown Center on Education and the Workforce).

Higher education, proper training, and experience serve us to obtain suitable jobs or start businesses in our areas of expertise. We can obtain suitable jobs according to our education and also get jobs with more responsibilities during the course of our careers. We may, however, find that we may not always get jobs that meet all our expectations.

Even though money, vacation and a health package are very important in a job, these are not the most important factors for employees, especially the new Y generation. People of this generation look to create their own new ideas and get them implemented. They expect open-mindedness from employers to accept their talent and appreciate what they contribute. They look for jobs with definite goals and responsibilities. In addition, they look for freedom at work and flexibility and trust in their performance.

People in Generation Y seek attention and recognition of their innovations. They also look for transparency in their performance. When they perform well and are trustworthy and innovative, they expect to be appreciated and paid well according to their performance.

Most of the time, we are fortunate to find jobs with good leaders and employers. Companies with good leadership, knowledge, understanding, and planning will help us to be nurtured properly during our careers. We will get opportunities to apply our knowledge to the fullest extent and develop ourselves to the highest level of performance without continuous stress. This is an ideal situation in which everyone will accomplish the most and be most productive. This is mutually beneficial to the people and the organizations they are associated with.

Our jobs become stressful for us when we take jobs beyond our capabilities or when we do not have good support systems. A good support system is defined as having proper tools and expert guidance from the leadership one is associated with. We may face situations in which we report to people with a lack of direction and knowledge of the business or whose egos interfere with the goals of the company. At times, the supervisor and employee may have conflicting chemistry. In such situations, we will be stressed and become less productive. We will feel discouraged and desperate due to a lack of team spirit.

Another factor to be faced is the intense competition with our peers to get ahead. Some of them take unprofessional steps to prove they are better than others. Sometimes, honesty and decency are compromised by their desire to get ahead at any cost.

Some managers treat employees like numbers and never feel sensitive to the needs of other people. They do not ask or allow employee input prior to making major decisions that affect their jobs. They manage by threats and fear. These kinds of environments create a lack of respect, trust and stress for everyone.

A successful manger will always have the full support and cooperation of the people who work with him or her and from his or her supervisors. It is important that key people are involved in decision-making processes so that they can implement plans with complete understanding. Because the people who implement the plan are involved in the planning process, there will be less resistance and better cooperation.

Greater resistance to management (those who represent the employer) will result in more breakdowns in communication. A lack of trust and respect will create conflicts and in turn encourage employees seeking outside help, which will result the formation of labor unions.

When employers and employees are in these kinds of situations, they must evaluate their situations and take corrective actions. They must try to reconcile the differences they have with their associates, colleagues, and supervisors. Everyone must be willing to negotiate and resolve all the problems. Successful people always negotiate, giving consideration to other parties' perspectives rather than their own.

A better understanding of everyone's needs makes reconciliation and settlement easier. Both employers and employees must never sacrifice honesty and integrity during these negotiations. However, they must keep their egos and arrogance in check during the settlement negotiations. Most negotiations fail due to a lack of honesty in negotiations.

Both employers and employees must have an attitude of giving and taking without losing the focus of negotiations. At the end of the settlements, everyone should feel like a winner. When they all feel like winners, this will create a better working relationship for the team, and the organization will benefit.

There are some instances, however, when both employers and employees cannot agree to reach a settlement. Since they cannot come to a settlement with direct negotiation, it is essential that they use a mediator, as agreed by both parties, to negotiate a settlement. They must be prepared to give and take to settle the disagreements.

Sometimes negotiations can take a long time. Even though negotiations are not directly conducted between the parties, the mediator can pursue both parties to make a few concessions each time. Ultimately, after lengthy negotiations, the mediator can reach a decision that is acceptable to all the parties. In the end, an agreement can be reached without major conflicts and mistrust. This process is definitely better than filing a lawsuit.

If everything fails, the next step is to take the case l to the courts for settlements. This is almost always a long process and can be expensive and stressful. The court decides in favor of one party or the other. This means that one party feels like a loser, and the other party feels like a winner.

In this situation, mistrust grows between the parties and creates an environment of long-term lack of cooperation. Most of the people do the minimum duties to get by without getting in trouble. In an event such as this, both parties lose their close working relationships resulting in financial losses for both parties.

This is not a healthy situation for either party involved. When there is mistrust, there will always be conflict. These types of environments are detrimental to all the people involved in the conflict. When they are in an environment filled with conflict and a lack of trust, they must try not to prolong the agony and plan for a change as soon as possible. They must take necessary actions so that, they will have opportunities to join different ventures and use their expertise. This will lead to a more productive and peaceful working environment.

When unnecessary stress is removed, they will enjoy their lives more and simultaneously contribute more to the people they are associated with and vice versa. This kind of environment will balance their lives. God is first, because He has provided everything for us and our families. A harmonious working environment is better than conflict and a lack of trust. They must always realize and understand that there is a higher purpose in life. They all look for peace and harmony.

"Finally, all of you live in harmony with one another, is sympathetic, love as brothers, be compassionate and humble. Do not pay evil with evil or insult with insult, but with blessing" (1 Peter 3:6 NIV).

Sometimes, people want to build their own businesses. The nature of the business must be understood to be successful. Such a venture requires versatility in various business areas. In addition to their expertise, they need to have sufficient capital and expert employees to build their businesses to be profitable. Depending on the business, the financial need may be six months to three years.

In order to be successful, business owners need to choose the right people, locations and build proper facilities or lease locations suitable for their businesses. They need to generate enough business, price it profitably, and execute in a timely fashion. We need all the above resources and the right combination of these necessary resources. It will not work if we have the best manager but not the right labor. All the resources have to be planned together and work together to make the enterprise successful. We need to change the mix of resources based on the circumstances and business cycles.

We must produce the right product at the right time at the right price and have proper, timely distribution to the right customer base to make an endeavor successful. If we do not work together, we will fail in our business enterprises. Egotistical and selfish people cannot be team players and usually create chaos within the team, leading to failure.

In the case of sole proprietors, they will have to manage all the details themselves. They need to manage their time effectively to assure that their customers can work around their schedules, or vice versa. Usually, juggling schedules will result in a lot of stress.

Since the owner is the only person to handle all the duties pertaining to the business, he or she will find that it is difficult to grow. This also applies if he or she is in the sole trader service business. Good time management is critical to short- and long-term business success.

In the event an owner plans to work in a non-service type of industry, he or she needs to have various expertise and resources. This person needs to have at least two to three years of capital for operating and capital expenditure needs. Usually it is difficult and stressful to raise or borrow capital. An owner will require a well thought out and well-written business plan to obtain sufficient finance.

In order to manage his or her business properly, and owner needs to have at least the following departments—sales, production, distribution, after-sales service, customer relations, and finance. He or she might need more departments based on the size of the business. There are many stresses that can result from not getting the right people and not getting enough income. In addition, well-managed organization is necessary for long term success. Many businesses fail because of poor organization and communication.

Even if the business has enough sales, it might have problems producing and distributing in a timely fashion. In addition to finding the right labor, it is important to have proper quality control. Improper quality control will result in customer dissatisfaction and returned sales. This will create both financial difficulties and customer retention problems. This is another major stress in business and reason for business failure.

Most organizations face stresses due to a lack of coordination between various departments. This can be corrected by having weekly meetings between all the departments. The chief officer must convene these meetings and establish proper guidelines, procedures, responsibilities, and timetables to facilitate smooth operation between the departments and total company operations. All procedures must be followed properly. Even after the complete execution of operation and sales functions, there can be problems related to customer satisfaction and after-sales service.

If all the products are properly executed, there can be still a problem of proper pricing and sending proper paperwork to customers in a timely fashion. Another problem a business faces is timely collection of all executed orders and accounts receivable. A major reason for business failure is improper financial management, resulting in excessive accounts receivable balances and excessive inventories. This will create financial stress, resulting in a shortfall of cash, which will affect the ability to meet day-to-day operating costs and other capital requirements.

Another major problem is making sure that the business is in compliance with all regulations. In business, there are lots of laws, challenges, and stresses related to preparing proper paperwork. It is difficult to find qualified people to file various required government reports. Most small businesses cannot afford to hire qualified people.

The small business operation is getting more complicated and cumbersome. However, when a business is settled and starts making a profit, it is more peaceful. The owner must continue to review profit margins on a regular basis to insure that all employees are performing well, loyal and trustworthy. Employees must be rewarded and treated properly so the owner can retain qualified employees for the long-term stability of the business.

Stress and Peace in Morals and Ethics

M orals can refer to rules and standards of conduct, good manners, character, and proper behaviors. The practice of good morals promotes the health and welfare of other humans or members of society. God gave Moses the Ten Commandments on Mount Sinai to serve as moral guidance for the human race. These laid down the principles of moral behavior. Obedience to these commandments will make our lives less stressful and more peaceful.

The Ten Commandments

1. You shall have no other gods.
2. You shall not make yourself in the form of anything in heaven.
2. You shall not misuse the name of the Lord.
4. Observe the Sabbath day.
5. Honor your father and mother.
6. You shall not murder.
7. You shall not commit adultery.
8. You shall not steal.
9. You shall not give false testimony against your neighbor.
10. You shall not covet your neighbor's wife.

No one is immune to sexual temptations or other immoral behaviors. Immoral behavior will weaken us physically, mentally, and spiritually and will hurt our spouses, children, parents, and close friends. We will lose the respect of many people we are closely associated with. When we break the commandment that says, "Thou shall not commit adultery," we grieve the God who came to redeem us. This also forces God to discipline us in various ways.

One of the major reasons for divorce is infidelity. Our guilty feelings will always plague our memories with flashbacks of the disrespectful behaviors. This could taint future intimacy with our spouses. We will feel that we have failed in our relationships with God. It is very important that we refrain from acting on temptations and establish strength within ourselves.

In addition to the above, we may face serious consequences of pregnancy, contracting AIDS, and other communicable diseases. We can also face lawsuits from the injured and can face major financial and emotional disasters. All these behaviors give us lots of stress and a loss of peace. So let us make sure that we do not act foolishly or impulsively to have a few minutes of pleasure. This will create years of living without respect, bad health, and the destruction of family life and will cause us to lose peace of mind.

"What comes out of man is what makes him unclean. For from within, out of men's hearts come evil thoughts, sexual immorality, theft, murder, adultery, greed, malice, deceit, lewdness, envy, slander, arrogance and folly" (Mark 7:21–22 NIV). So let us practice morality and live with less stress and more peace.

Stress and Peace in Marriage

Marriage is a social union between people called spouses, legally approved by law. Once one has finished his or her education and settled into a career, it is time to think about having a life partner to share his or her accomplishments with. Before committing to marrying a person, one must understand that everyone is unique, and no one is perfect.

As a tradition in Christian weddings, we usually have two candles representing two unique individuals. During the wedding ceremony, each person will take his or her candle and light a single candle. This represents that both are different people with different backgrounds and characteristics that plan to live in unity. It does not mean that both of them lose their independence or unique characteristics as individuals.

This is symbolic; however, both spouses must become interdependent in all their future actions. All actions must be taken in unison and not independently. This will create an atmosphere of better trust, communication, and peace. Marriage is a lifetime commitment between husband and wife. "Married woman is bound to her husband as long as he lives" (Romans 7:2 NIV). "Husbands love your wives just as Christ loved the Church and gave himself for her" (Ephesians 5:25 NIV).

In addition to our own relationships, we must understand that our new relationships will automatically create additional extended family and circles of friends. We have to recognize the unique characteristics of everyone we deal with. We need to make adjustments to accommodate the behavior and lifestyles of different people.

During the course of our lives, we have to make many sacrifices and adjustments to establish proper relationships with the members of one another's families and friends. Sometimes we have to go through short-term stress to accomplish this.

The more accommodating we are the better life becomes. We experience less stress and more peace—beyond our imagination—in our family lives. We must always understand that our family lives are not only about us, but also about all the other people involved in our lives.

Sometimes we need to stretch our behaviors to accommodate everyone's needs. We must be mature and grow well together without being selfish. Selfishness will create conflicts and turmoil in life. It is very important to build excellent relationships with our loved ones. Together, we can succeed. Otherwise we will create a lot of stress in our lives. Stress and a lack of relationships can deteriorate our quality of life with our loved ones.

We will never be happy and peaceful without proper relationships and understanding. We must always settle our differences by forgiving and forgetting wrong deeds. Otherwise we will grow up without a good support system, feel left out and lonely. A survey shows that by forgiving and forgetting wrong deeds, the number of patients in hospitals and other care facilities can be decreased by 50 percent (Research was supported by a grant from the Templeton Foundation to Drs. Jones and Lawler for study of forgiveness). We must free our minds from animosity, anxiety and vengeance to lead peaceful lives.

Listed below are few criteria for lasting happiness and peaceful relationships. We mentioned earlier that every one of us is unique. However, building strong relationships together makes life happier and allows us to lead more peaceful lives.

Husbands and wives must always communicate openly and establish trust for all their actions. The journey of life must be carried on in total faith and without any secrets between the spouses. Spouses must only have mutual friends and never have friends who belong to one person or the other. All friends must be trustworthy to both spouses.

Occasionally, you may have some time out with your friends to have your own space. But all these actions must be done with mutual understanding and full cooperation of spouses. Spouses may disagree on some issues but must take action in unison to build an understanding on all issues. We must never go to sleep at night without discussing and settling all disagreements. We must learn to forgive and forget each other's weaknesses.

We must learn to live within our means and set aside enough resources for our future. We must not spend all our income on day-to-day living. We must make it a habit to set aside at least 10 percent for God to help the needy and 10 percent for our retirement needs. If we started saving late in life, we have to save a greater percentage of our income. It is important but what we save and what we make. We need to set aside enough funds for the future to insure that we can have the lifestyles we are accustomed to.

We must always learn to forgive and forget each other's faults and weakness. We must build our lives on each other's strengths and never take advantage of each other's weaknesses. We must assist each other to correct our weaknesses and enjoy our strengths. We must always understand that no one is perfect. We must never criticize or negatively judge each other. We must learn to accommodate and accept each other's special interests and needs.

True love for each other must always be sincere, unconditional, and sacrificial. When we love each other unconditionally, we can only grow stronger together and not apart. In order to have strong relationships and growth, we must always give each other enough personal space.

We must make sure that our actions never hurt the feelings of other people. If they are hurt unintentionally, we must discuss the matter and correct it once and for all. We must ask for and accept forgiveness to strengthen our lives. This action will lead to less stress and more peace.

We must always complement and appreciate each other. We must not criticize each other, especially in front of other people. All disagreements or misunderstandings must be discussed and settled prior to bedtime. It is essential to have proper sleep for a healthy life. We are not perfect human beings, and accordingly, unpleasant things and mistakes can happen in our lives. We must learn from these mistakes and correct our behaviors accordingly.

We must always be trustworthy. We must not take any actions that will create any kind of mistrust between us. We must always understand that we are life partners and are responsible for each other's actions and consequences. We need to support each other throughout married life. We must always be peaceful, despite stress, through mutual trust, understanding, and unconditional and truthful love for each other. Together, we can make peaceful lives for ourselves and our children.

We must continuously strengthen our relationships by mutually keeping romance active. We must do small things to maintain our love for each other. It is nice to send some loving notes or go out for a special dinner at a favorite restaurant. We must always remember each other's special days and needs. It should be similar to the romance we had during the early periods of marriage. We must always respect each other's feelings and not nag each other. We must continue to be honest with each other at all times.

We must always be willing to constructively criticize each other and accept each other's criticisms to improve ourselves. We must never be defensive when receiving constructive criticism. We must always compromise rather than create conflicts. We must always share responsibilities pleasantly and consider that these are our duties; sharing these duties allows us to reduce stress and increase peace.

"For this reason a man will leave his father and mother and be united with his wife and the two will become one flesh. So they are no longer two, but one. Therefore what God has joined together, let man not separate" (Matthew 19:5–6 NIV).

Stress and Peace of having Children.

Once a couple establishes a strong relationship, they may consider extending their relationship by having a family. We have children to extend our families, share our accomplishments, and have pleasant lives. We must never have children and expect that the children will alleviate our conflicts and strengthen our relationships. As a matter of fact, if we do not have trust and strong relationships between each other, children might further strain the relationships.

We all know that children are a major, lifelong commitment. We need to take more responsibilities and must work together more closely to raise the children properly. The children will take a lot of our time and resources, so it is essential that both partners commit to the betterment of the children. Parents have to sacrifice many things in life to accommodate children's needs. Unless we make a total commitment to the children, they will have a hard time coping with life and growing properly. When they see our pleasant and cooperative lifestyles, they can follow and build their own lifestyles more easily.

When we feel strongly about our relationships, we are ready to take on more responsibilities and have more children. Children are the best source of happiness. This happiness comes with considerable commitments and responsibilities. When we see the face of a newborn child, life takes us in a completely new direction. In order to nurture children to the fullest extent, both parents have to dedicate themselves completely. Our priorities in our lives have to be rearranged to insure that the children get our full attention and we can nurture them for proper growth.

Until a child is born, spouses accommodate each other and build other relationships. After the child is born, they may not in a position to do everything they did before. Sometimes we feel that we missed many opportunities we had before because of our focus on our new responsibilities. We might feel stretched beyond our abilities.

This might create a higher stress level within the family for a short period. We must never forget that with the blessing of God, we brought these responsibilities upon ourselves. We must be prepared to give unconditional, sacrificial love and attention to the well-being of our children.

It is essential that parents share responsibilities and decisions. We cannot shirk our responsibilities to our children. Our efforts should be to raise the children together to the fullest extent possible. Most parents often feel that their children are the best in the world. Before children were born, they do not experience these kinds of feelings and responsibilities.

We must seek guidance and help to insure that the children get our dedication, love, care, and trust. We may not be perfect, but we should assure them that we always do our best. An atmosphere of love, respect and trust is very important to help children grow up properly. We must always act in unison to guide and discipline our children. We must never overrule the other person's decision. When in doubt, parents should consult each other.

Parents must make sure that we nurture children with love and care and not by fear. Children are helpless without us and completely dependent on us. We must be completely committed to the growth of our children. We must guide them through this imperfect life. We must make them respectful of us and assist them in freely discussing their strengths and weakness with us. Children must be encouraged to discuss their daily activities with us without any fear of reprimand.

Parents' expectations of their children's performance must be high. Children must be disciplined for bad behaviors but praised for their good behaviors. They must be disciplined by parents taking away their privileges for short periods. We must never take away their privileges for a prolonged period. This is to make them aware that there are consequences for their bad behaviors all throughout their lives. But they can correct their wrong actions and get positive results.

We must praise children in public and discipline them in private in a calm and quiet manner. Children are helpless and physically weaker than us. We must never discipline them by screaming or giving physical punishment. They must be given well-rounded nurturing physically, mentally, and spiritually.

Children must be guided well to live within their means and taught how to manage their time and resources. They must be taught to stretch themselves for optimum accomplishments and performance. They must understand the importance of education and knowledge. They must understand that their knowledge is power that is never to be abused.

Children must be taught to be compassionate and helpful to others in need. They must be taught that their God-given talents and resources are not only for themselves but also to help others in need. They must be taught to be honest, of high integrity, and never greedy. They must always show humility, respect, and love for others.

It is essential that parents nurture the children to become part of the family and society. Parents should participate in all the children's activities while they are growing up. It is very important that children are given good guidance and discipline. If at an early age, they understand how to manage their resources properly, it will make their lives easier when they become independent.

Children must understand that they cannot have everything in life, just like parents cannot have everything in life. We must discuss our financial resources, strengths, and weaknesses with them. The family that prays together and dines together will grow better together. Children must be prepared to face their stressful lives with peace and tranquility.

Children must always interface with parents' families and friends. We must make them understand that despite of all our efforts, there are some friends and family members who do not always cooperate and try to create conflict. They must also understand that we can never make everyone happy and peaceful. We do the best we can and offer them truth, love, and peace.

We might come across some people who do not know how to accept our love. Jesus sent disciples and advised them:

"If anyone will not welcome you or listen to your words, shake the dust off your feet when you leave that home or town" (Matthew 10:14 NIV).

In our lifetimes, we might have to change some friends and members of the family to be peaceful at home. We must make children understand that true love and relationships are mutually beneficial for everyone. However, selfishness can lead to loneliness. Once we accept all these responsibilities and accomplish positive results, our lives become less stressful, and we will have more peace.

Stress and Peace of Divorce

We have previously discussed that we must strengthen our partnerships prior to having any children. We must develop unconditional and truthful love for each other. We must practice true love as written in Bible: "Love, is patient, kind, does not envy, does not boast, is not proud, not rude, not self-seeking, not easily angered, keeps no record of wrongs, does not delight in evil, rejoices with truth, always protects, always trusts, always hopes, always preserves and never fails" (1 Corinthians 13:4–7 NIV).

If we practice true love, we will always grow together. We must always be there for each other in prosperity and poverty, health and sickness, and at all times. In spite of all these commitments, sometimes, we grow apart. Why does this happen? There are many reasons why we do not grow together. One out of three marriages fails in this country. The main reasons for divorce are lack of commitment (73 percent), arguing (56 percent), infidelity (55 percent), marrying too young (46 percent), unrealistic expectations (45 percent), and a lack of love and trust (Dr. William H. Doherty. "Marriage is a Counter Cultural Act in a throwaway Society").

Sometimes we are not grateful to God or content with what we have. We always want more and do not know how to enjoy what we have. As human beings, we are never satisfied with what we have and always want more. There is nothing wrong with stretching your capabilities and taking on short-term stress to earn more and have more. We should not, however, be unhappy and jealous because of what other people have that we do not. We must never forget the basic fact that all of us are meant to complement one another.

We must never forget the promises we made during our marriages that we will be together until death parts us. We do not always follow the steps we have previously discussed for strengthening our marriages. This will result in us growing apart and becoming more self-centered and isolated, resulting in irreconcilable differences and a lack of trust and respect. Once we lose our trust and respect for each other, we assume that we would be happier living apart.

We must realize that divorce will separate us and our children and destroy the roofs we have all lived under. Those who divorce also may break some relationships and friendships they had built together. This will also apply to our children and generations to come. Before couples separate and decide to divorce, they must go to counseling to understand each other better and take corrective actions. They must take some time to think about and evaluate the consequences of divorce. We must always try to alleviate this situation for the betterment of all.

The consequences of divorce are very serious, especially when children are involved. These selfish actions of ours affect children adversely. Please make sure that divorce is a friendly separation and assure children that their needs are always our first priority. We must assure our children that they will not be put in the middle of our problems and disagreements. As a matter of fact, we must go out of our way to insure that the physical separation of the parents will not affect their closeness to the children. We must always make them understand that they are not the reason for separation. This is purely the parents' own fault, and they will always be there for the children, even though they are not together.

Divorce creates stress between some of the friends and in relationships with people they had established during their married lives. We must act as mature individuals and never use children for our advantage. Children must be supported by both parents, just like before the divorce. Our unstable behavior will create instability for the children. Children are already affected adversely by not having their parents under the same roof. We must always be a part of all the children's activities after the divorce. We must make sure that we are available for them. Children should never have to force themselves to choose between their parents.

Most people are affected adversely and will experience physical, mental, and financial stress due to separation and divorce. Divorce establishes dual residences and dual expenses, causing financial and emotional stress for both parents and children. Most of the time, divorce will reduce the standard of living for both parents and children.

Physical and emotional stress can cause sickness and loneliness. It is important that parents celebrate special occasions of the children together. We must cooperate and celebrate together during special events, such as graduations, family get-togethers, and other events. We must be there for the children on every important occasion. We must always try to grow together.

In the event parents marry again, we must make sure that children are involved in the process and all celebrations. We must make sure that new spouses are properly introduced to the children. Children will always be resistant to sharing their mothers or fathers with other spouse. We must make sure that new spouses spend time together with children and make everyone comfortable. Children do not always understand adults' loneliness and need for a partner. All spouses must be friendly and cooperative for the sake of children. We must all grow together, even though we live separately.

Finally, divorce causes economic loss and reduces productivity for the individuals. Divorce can be reduced if you find happiness within yourself rather than depending on your spouse for all happiness. We must have our own times with other friends and relations. These interactions give us an opportunity to meet and understand that other people's lives are not always perfect.

Please try to understand that living together is more pleasant and practical than living separately. In the long run, it creates a lot of stability if we are able to adjust a few things in life and enjoy it together. Let us all try to learn to accommodate and forgive each other's weaknesses and develop strength as couples. Let us not forget that nobody is perfect, and our imperfections create problems that must be forgiven and forgotten. Time will cure all problems and alienations. We must follow the definition of love in 1 Corinthians to have a better understanding of each other and behave responsibly.

> God has called us to live in peace. How do you know wife, weather you will save your husband? Or how do you know husband, whether you will save your wife. Nevertheless each one should retain the place in life that Lord assigned to him and to which God has called him. (1 Corinthians 7:15–17 NIV)

The spiritual life will give us belief, hope, and love. These things will give us less stress, more happiness, and peace. Let us begin depending on God rather than human beings to be more peaceful.

Stress and Peace in Finance

Financial peace is very important for a stable life for us, our families, and the society we live in. If we do not have financial responsibility and stability, we will always be stressed. We must always maximize the utilization of our talents and resources to produce maximum resources while we are gainfully employed and able to do so.

We must never forget that our lives are not only for us but that we need to share with less fortunate people. God created us with a purpose, to share our talents and resources with others who are less fortunate. God created every one of us with different talents to complement each other and not to compete. We must never forget that one day; we could be on the receiving end rather than the giving end.

Everyone's financial resources, investment results, pension plans, retirement benefits, retirement ages, inheritances, and health situations are different. These guidelines listed below will provide us with some general idea of prudent financial management for a normal family while we are employed or in business. We must always live within our means, set aside portions of our earnings for income after retirement, and contribute portions of our earnings to God's plan for us to help others.

We must always understand that God gave these resources to us, and He can take them away any time He wants. Most of us are employed gainfully for about twenty-five to forty years. Most of us have to retire at around sixty-five years, and our regular earnings will cease as of that date. Based on life expectancy, we can expect to live ten to thirty years after retirement.

People must have enough income to maintain the lifestyles they are used to after retirement. Most of our day-to-day expenses will continue after retirement, and our regular incomes will cease. Even if the homes we live in are paid off, the taxes, insurance, maintenance, etc. will continue. We will still have our automobiles and travel expenses. As a matter of fact, we might need more money for travel, because we will have more leisure time that we did not have while we were actively working. Our total expenses can be 60–70 percent of pre-retirement expenses.

If we are not prepared, our retirement lives can be very stressful and troublesome. We can become more stressed if we need to provide additional support for our children or close family members and friends in need. Stress can increase due to sicknesses or disasters beyond our control. We can be blessed, however, with responsible and supportive children and family members and friends who might take care of our needs, resulting in a peaceful life.

Budget

Managing our resources properly is very important to lessen stresses in our lives. In order to control our spending habits, we must prepare budgets based on our incomes. In addition, we must keep track of our expenditures as compared to our budgets.

In the event we are not good bookkeepers, we must pay cash for our expenses and prepare separate envelopes for each category of expenses. We must always carry these envelopes with us and pay our expenses from these envelopes. When the money is exhausted in the designated envelope, we must cease spending any more monies for this category of expense.

In case of emergency, we can borrow from one category for another category. But do not make a habit of swapping funds between the envelopes unless it is a budget error. If there is a budget error, we must correct the budget categories. We must, however, never borrow additional money to cover the expenses. Any amount not spent during the month must be put aside in an emergency fund. We must set aside enough money for emergency fund needs, which should be about six months of our gross expenses.

If we continue to manage our expenses very prudently, we may be able to save even from the budgeted expenses. We must deposit these monies into long-term investments, Roth IRA funds, annuity funds, or other investments. This decision is based on our short- or long-term financial needs. After retirement, we will be able to draw the funds without paying any additional taxes if we saved the money in a Roth IRA, because it was deposited as an after-tax fund.

This budget schedule is only a basic guideline and applies to most families earning average incomes. The intent of this schedule is to insure that we do not spend more money than we make. This guideline may vary depending on our inheritance, retirement income, and other circumstances. Depending on our situations, we can adjust the money in each category as long as it does not exceed the total income. You must review this every year and adjust the budget accordingly based on your income changes.

Since our economy is faltering and our industrial base is eroding, we may not be able to contribute enough funding for Medicare, Medicaid, Social Security, and other benefits. In order to continue balance the deficit in funds available, we might end up in getting reduced benefits in future. This applies to both private and public organizations. We must realize that in the future, we will be held responsible for our own retirement needs. In some cases, we are held responsible now.

You will note that no money is provided for education in the budget. If our children cannot get scholarships or student loans, we need to review and revise our budgets accordingly. As previously discussed, financial stress for parents can be reduced by children taking more responsibility for their own future education needs at an early age. The children must focus on their studies rather than wasting their valuable time doing irresponsible activities that give them short-term satisfaction.

Children must stretch themselves to the best of their abilities to support their parents. They can receive scholarships, get assistance, and do part-time work. They should get involved in the annual family budget preparation. The better they understand the financial status of the family, the more responsible they become. This is an added incentive for children to understand the family finances. It is very important that everyone in the family woks together to reduce stress and increase happiness and peace.

The last thing we want to do is provide everything children ask for without their knowing the sacrifices parents have to make to do so. In the event parents are short of money, it is very important that children understand that. They must learn that no one can have everything he or she wants. We must teach them how to accept the refusal of their demands. We must make them understand that we will try to meet their needs but not all their wants.

The top priority for children is to focus on their studies when they are young and plan for their future education. It is essential that parents make them understand the importance of the commitment they have to make to their educations to have comfortable lives of their own. If children maximize their abilities and do their best, they can get assistance and scholarships, resulting in less stress for themselves and their parents.

If children cannot get educational assistance, they may have to work part-time while studying. This is a possibility children have to understand at an early age. It is up to them to be responsible for their actions and their futures. Working and attending college may result in some stress for a short period, but the end results will be well worth it. They will be able to enjoy the long-term positive impact of their educations.

The children's participation in family needs is also an indication that children are concerned about and love their parents. They do not need to waste their parents' resources on short-term pleasures. This will give parents more comfort and less stress and improve relations with and appreciation for their children. When the family works together as a unit in all its pursuits, members can create strong, loving, and caring families. Relationships between parents and children will become stronger, reduce stress, and increase peace in the family. Children will love, respect, and appreciate their parents more in the long run. They will understand and appreciate their parents even better when they become parents and are responsible for their own children.

The schedule listed below is only a guideline and will vary depending upon each individual's unique situation. We must never spend more than our incomes to reduce stress.

Description	Budget Percent	Estimated Amount
Income	100	100,000
Home	25	25,000
Transportation	8	8,000
Food	10	10,000
Utilities	5	5,000
Entertainment	1	1,000
Emergency Fund	5	5,000
Personal Expenses	2	2,000
Savings/Retirement	10	10,000
Help Others	10	10,000
Taxes	15	15,000
Health/Life Insurance	5	5,000
Miscellaneous	4	4,000
Total Expenses	100	100,000

However, we must always make sure that we put away enough savings for expenses after retirement. If we do not set aside enough monies for our expenses after retirement, financial hardship will be a major stress during our retirements. We cannot live in joy and peace if we do not prepare for our retirements. When we are younger and earn good incomes, we tend to minimize our future retirement needs. We all know that we have to set aside enough income for our retirement from our earnings while we work. The younger we start, the easier it will be to meet our retirement goals.

Most people, however, while working, do not think about or plan for life after retirement. They all feel that they have many years left to save. Many of them do not understand that it is difficult to save and easy to spend. Most of them do not think about getting old and the need to support them-selves without any earned income. They do not think or understand that they need at least 60 to 70 percent of their last five years' average spending per year to maintain their lifestyles in retirement.

My recommendation is to set aside at least 10 percent of their income the day they start earning. Another way to save money for retirement is to set aside 50 percent of the raises they get each year.

Children must realize that they will have families of their own, and they must be prepared to be responsible for them. They must understand in most cases that their parents' support or inheritance may not be there when they retire. They need to understand that their parents may need help from them after they retire.

In addition, when you have joint income, you must try to live on one person's income. This will help when couples take care of their children when they are young. The more parents spend time with their children, the more the children will understand and realize the importance of their parents' love and affection.

Children must also learn that the material things are not as important as love and affection. Children will be better prepared for their futures when they experience a lot of love and affection. We can always buy material things later but provide lot of love and affection when they are young.

Home Purchases and Leasing

There are many people in the world who never own their own homes. They live in rented apartments for life or live with others. Some people are satisfied with the minimum necessities of life, such as three meals a day or a minimum set of clothes. There are many people who go to sleep without any food. Most of them cannot even think about ever owning their own homes.

In the US, 67 percent of people own their homes. We have seen an increase in the size and square footage of homes since 1970s. The increase in the average size of homes in the US resulted in an increase in housing costs. Based on US census data, listed below are the average sizes of homes in US, which vary from state to state. However, in 2012, we see a slight decrease in the average size of homes. If we continue this trend, it would be a tremendous advantage to homeowners to reduce their payments and live within their means.

Year	Square Footage
1975	1,650
1985	1,800
1995	2,100
2005	2,450
2010	2,400

Owning a home is an accomplishment for everyone. This will establish stability for the family. Those who own a home feel like a part of the community and establish orderly social interactions with neighbors and the community as a whole. Home ownership gives us freedom to choose our own needs and decorations in our homes. We have freedom to choose our own surroundings rather than be under the control of landlords.

For most people, a home is the largest personnel investment they make in their lives. Before buying a home, there are few important points to be considered.

We must plan on staying for a long period. When we sell homes, we must be able to make a profit to recover the closing cost of financing, title fees, court fees, and down payments for new homes. We must establish good credit ratings, because the mortgage rates depend on the credit scores and our ability to make monthly payments. We must not finance 100 percent of a house. We must try to make down payments of 20–30 percent.

We must try to buy homes in good condition, in good locations, and in good school districts to maintain the home value. We must get expert opinions about points versus mortgage rates. We can get the information from financial planners and trustworthy lenders. Make sure to get preapproval to determine the maximum home payment you can afford to pay on a monthly basis. This will avoid losing the opportunity to buy a suitable home when you find a home you really like if the price is not in your approval limit. You must always have a home inspection for a qualified building inspector to confirm that there are no major issues with the home.

For most of us, the biggest expenditure we have is payment for the homes we live in. It is important that homes are paid off and free from any mortgage prior to retirement. We must make sure that our home loans are sufficiently insured and will be paid off in case of a partner's death or disability. We will still continue to spend on taxes, insurance, repairs, maintenance, utilities, homeowner's dues, day-to-day living expenses, transportation etc.

We should always buy homes that we can afford to live in for life time. We understand that people have become more mobile due to job opportunities and new housing developments. Some people buy homes to keep up with friends who moved into bigger homes. We must understand that we do not have to move because our friends left the area. We should know that true friendship comes from what we are and not from what we have.

If material possession is the only reason for our friendship, we must know that it is not true friendship. The story of prodigal son in the Bible

(Luke 15:11–32) illustrates this.

The prodigal son who squandered all the wealth inherited from his father lost all his friends. He found out the hard way that they were not his true friends. When he returned home with nothing, his father accepted him the way he was because of the true love for him as his son. When we have resources available, we must manage them safely and always set aside for future needs. We must live with joy and peace but never be wasteful.

This brings up the important question of how many years to finance when we buy our homes. The most important criterion is to buy a home that you can afford to make payments on without stress. Financing must depend on age and income at the time of acquisition of the home. You must never take a loan beyond retirement age. You must be free from the loan when your main source of income has ceased. This is because your income will be reduced substantially after retirement. Most other expenses will continue to increase every year depending on cost-of-living factors.

The most commonly used financing period is thirty years. If you buy a home at the age of thirty, you may finance it for thirty years. If you buy the home at forty years, you must not finance it for more than twenty-five years. If you buy at fifty years, finance it for no more than for fifteen years. If you buy a home at sixty years, you must not finance for more than five years or pay cash. You will pay substantially less interest expense if you can finance your home for a shorter period. Based on the payment schedule, you must decide how long to finance your home.

I strongly recommend no more than fifteen years for a home mortgage, even if you buy when you are thirty years old. For example, if you finance the loan for $300,000 at 10 percent for fifteen years, you pay only $3,224 per month. If you finance the same for thirty years, the payment will be $2,633 per month. You pay only $591 more per month for fifteen years.

The total amount you will pay for thirty years is $947,880. The total amount you will pay for fifteen years will be $580,320. This is a net savings of $367,560. This is a net savings of $2,042 per month for fifteen years. In other words, if you reduce the financing period, your savings will be greater than most any other investment you make.

Listed below are schedules showing the loan amount, interest rates, and the actual payment for different rates. This does not include property taxes and property insurance.

Mortgage Payment Schedule

$100,000 Loan at 5%

Monthly Payment	Total Payment	Years
$537	$193,000	30
$791	$142,000	15
$1,061	$127,000	10
$1,887	$113,000	5

$100,000 Loan at 10%

Monthly Payment	Total Payment	Years
$878	$316,000	30
$1,075	$193,000	15
$1,322	$159,000	10
$2,125	$127,000	5

$300,000 Loan at 5%

Monthly Payment	Total Payment	Years
$1,610	$580,000	30
$2,372	$427,000	15
$3,182	$382,000	10
$5,661	$340,000	5

$300,000 Loan at 10%

Monthly Payment	Total Payment	Years
$2,633	$948,000	30
$3,224	$580,000	15
$3,965	$476,000	10
$6,374	$382,000	5

We must understand that in addition to the monthly payments, there are other costs, such as taxes, insurance, utilities, repairs, maintenance, and various other expenses. Depending on the community, you may have to pay additional homeowner's dues and other common area costs.

If the monthly payment of mortgage, including insurance and taxes exceeds more than the amount shown in the budget guideline (preferably less than 25 percent of your income), it means that you are buying a home beyond your financial means. This kind of excessive cost can cause a lot of stress for you and your family for a long time. You will have to sacrifice other normal activities in life to accommodate the house payments. This will result in an inability to enjoy your home and relax with your family and friends. In addition, you will always feel stressed to make payments on time.

You must never buy a home if you have to work multiple jobs to pay for it. This is a distressing sign that you cannot really afford the home and are living beyond your means and needs. You must always consider what happens if one of the spouses is not able to work because of job loss, sickness, or death. It is always better to budget your house payment based on one person's income.

As a general practice, most of us do not prepare a budget. If we spend according to the guidelines above, we would be without major financial stress and live in peace. In the event a spouse gets sick or is unemployed, the family with better plan will be able to manage its financial matters with less stress. In addition, in the event full-time attention is needed for children or anyone else due to sickness or another reason, one spouse can quit work and spends quality time with the family.

You must never take an equity loan on the house for day-to-day needs. In case of emergency, if you have to take an equity loan, you must take a loan or refinance the loan based on your age, as shown above. Please make sure that the total loan payment for the home never exceeds 25 percent of your income, including the refinanced amount or new loan. If the payment exceeds 25 percent, you will experience stress and a lack of peace. Again, I emphasize the need to pay off the home prior to retirement.

Traditionally, second homes have always been a good long-term investment when the home value appreciated more than the cost of living index. This consistent appreciation of the value helped people rent their second homes without major cash loss for a long time. This is because the rent increases annually with no increase in the monthly mortgage payments. This will result in long term positive cash flow.

However, cash flow can be adversely affected by the increase in property taxes and property insurance. Due to the economic problems we currently face, many real estate investments have become riskier. Most of the time, when we have disposable income, we buy homes to reduce the tax liability by showing a loss on rental property or taking reduction of interest and taxes on the second homes.

When you plan to purchase a second home or rental home for tax purposes and a long term-investment, you must insure that you do not incur continuous negative cash flow. You must always make sure that your negative cash flow for a rental home does not create stress in your day-to-day life.

It is also very important to calculate that your total negative cash flow incurred on a monthly basis never exceeds the tax break you receive and the appreciation of the property at the time of sale. If you do not accomplish a positive cash flow at the time of the disposal of the property, it is not considered a good investment. Investment value also depends on having a good tenant who maintains the property well. In the event you have an irresponsible tenant, the property could be destroyed, which will further deteriorate the investment value.

Buying or Leasing Automobiles

The basic purpose of an automobile is to provide safe, reliable day-to-day transportation. Next to a home, the next major purchase is an automobile. We all know that the value of an automobile depreciates faster than that of most of our assets. The value of the vehicle can go down as much as 50 percent in two to three years.

Most well-maintained automobiles are reliable sources of transportation for more than one hundred thousand miles and a life of more than ten years. We must make sure that all the preventive maintenance is done in a timely fashion to avoid major repairs. Maintenance cost is very minimal compared to that of major repairs or the replacement cost of the automobile.

Many people, however, buy new automobiles as prestige items. As long as it does not create any financial stress, it is okay to buy a new automobile anytime. Otherwise, you must buy a vehicle and finance it for no more than two to three years. Make sure that the annual payment does not exceed the financial budget guideline. If the cost of maintenance and the monthly payment exceeds the budget criteria, you are buying an automobile beyond your means.

The best way to purchase an automobile is with cash. When you are young and cannot afford to pay for a new automobile, you must buy an inexpensive, good used car costing less than your budget guideline.

You must save the difference in the monthly payment of a new car for upgrading to the next car. You will be pleasantly surprised to see that you will save enough money to upgrade the car every two to three years. If you keep upgrading like this, you will be able to buy an excellent late-model used car within a few years. You will be able to save a substantial amount of hard earned money.

There may be a disadvantage to a buy a new car if you have an accident immediately after acquisition. The insurance company may try to settle for blue book value rather than the loan balance, which is usually higher than the blue book value due to depreciation.

We must also teach our children how to manage finances from an early age. We must teach them about financial resources from childhood to make them more responsible when they become adults. If we continue to manage our finances prudently, we will not experience any major financial stress, resulting in more peaceful lives.

Leasing allows us to drive new cars every two or three years. Leasing is an option when we feel that we have to have new cars but cannot afford the monthly payments for the purchase of a new car. Leased car payments are usually less than financing the purchase of a new car. Most of the time, the lease payment and interest rate on a leased car, is more favorable than that of a new car.

In the event we drive more than the stipulated lease miles, the excess miles might cost us $0.15–$0.25 per mile. If we know that we will use more miles than allowed by lease terms, we must buy excess miles at the beginning of the lease, which is usually much lower rate than regular mileage costs. The end of lease, if we can pay for additional miles without at regular rate, we must lease the car based on lowest usage per year. This will give us a reduced lease rate.

Credit Cards

Credit cards are issued by credit card companies, such as banks, other financial and retail institutions, authorizing us to use them with a dollar limit for our purchases of goods and services. Sometimes, credit card companies issue credit cards without verifying the credit worthiness of the applicants. All credit card companies are competing for a share of the market without considering that, some people they issue credit cards to do not know how to manage the credit cards prudently. Most people have a tendency to buy more than they need when buying with credit cards.

We must make sure that we always pay the full balance due at the end of the month when it is due. If we are not able to pay the balance due in full, it means that we purchased beyond our means or had unexpected emergency needs. This will create a shortage of funds available for future needs, and we will always be under financial stress. In addition, we must think about the extra money we pay due to late fees and exorbitant interest rates.

The income for credit card companies is a very small charge for the merchants, and interest and penalties they collect from the credit card users. Credit cards must be used as a convenient way to pay for goods and services and not as financial loan instruments. The average credit card balance in a household in US is over $15,000, which is usually more than 25 percent of the average family income. The total outstanding credit card balance is over $800 billion.[4]

The average credit card balance of undergraduate students is more than $3,000. Student loan balances total more than a trillion dollars at an average of over $26,000 per student in 2012. However, 10 percent of student loans are over $54,000, and 3 percent of students owe more than $100,000 (National Student Loan Data System).

We know that the amount of a loan balance increases due to added interest. This kind of loan structure creates a lot of stress for students and parents. This situation is getting worse due to our economic conditions, increased tuition fees, and increased unemployment. Credit card institutions made a profit of over $18 billion in 2011 (Credit Card Industries Profit Statistics by BCS Alliance). This is the money they collected from merchants and credit card holders for interest and late fees.

We must be very cautious how we use our credit cards. In addition to buying unnecessary stuff, we put ourselves in a position of not being able to pay the full balance each month. As discussed earlier, this will result in increasing the amount we owe plus exorbitant interest and late fees. In the long run, these excessive purchases and resulting balances, if not paid in a timely fashion, will result in bad credit scores. Bad credit scores will affect interest rates on mortgages and other loans.

Another important aspect of using a credit card is protecting the credit card. We can insure credit cards for loss and theft. We must be very cautious about how we manage our credit card. Any time we use credit cards, we must make sure that we clear the sale by pressing the "clear" button to avoid misuse by others. When cashiers return your credit cards, you must verify that you receive your card and not an expired credit card that belongs to another person.

If you are an impulse buyer, you must not use credit cards. The impulse buyer must make it a practice to delay the execution of purchases for at least twenty-four hours. By practicing this on a regular basis, we can change the habit of impulse purchases and reduce the number of unnecessary things we buy. This will also reduce financial stress. Another way to control impulse buying is to use a debit card for all purchases. This will limit your purchasing power to the extent of the available cash balance in the bank. Most of the time, we can get a better price if we buy with cash.

If buying is a major source of happiness, you have a psychological problem and must consider consulting a counselor. Happiness is within you and not created by buying material stuff. The happiness produced by the acquisition of material things is very short-term. Most of us will realize that the stuff we buy is usually not needed and only a spur-of-the-moment purchase.

Due to excessive purchases, most people are running out of space in their closets and homes. One of the fastest-growing businesses in the US is the storage business. Since its inception in 1972, it has grown to 22 billion-dollar business in 2011 (Self Storage Association). In the long run, most of the excessive items we buy and possess are stored at these places. Items in the storage units are rarely used and seldom retrieved. Many families suffer due to excessive purchases that create financial stress and a lack of peace.

Sometimes, we do not realize or understand that we are compulsive buyers or hoarders. Hoarding appears to be a psychological disorder that causes a habit of excessive acquisition and unwillingness to discard anything. In addition to creating a filthy place to live, it is also unhygienic. Hoarding is when we buy things for fear of running out of items and feeling deprived. We buy more than one of a similar item because of a fear that the item will break down or not be available again. This also can cause depression, anxiety, or attention deficit and hyperactive disorders. Excessive buying can create a lot of stress for us and people closely associated with us. We must seek help to create better lives for ourselves and our loved ones. Proper management of our purchases will give us more space in our houses, more peace of mind, and happiness and reduce financial stress.

Insurance

Life insurance is absolutely essential for everyone for protection against unexpected circumstances. When we are young and our families are growing, there is a greater need to protect ourselves and prepare for emergencies. If a spouse dies, the other spouse has to take care of all family needs. It is essential that we carry life insurance policies to cover the deficit in income for five to ten years. This amount varies from person to person. We must buy what we need to sustain our lifestyles until we resettle our lives.

The loss of a dear one causes major emotional stress for the surviving partner, children, and family members. The last thing we need during these periods is to worry about immediate financial needs. Once we cover the financial areas of responsibility, we can focus on other issues.

It is also my recommendation that a person buy term insurance rather than whole life insurance. If we can afford whole life insurance premiums, we must take the difference in premiums between the two and invest in long-term annuities, mutual funds, or other investments. The basic purpose of life insurance is to have an income to sustain us for a few years until we are resettled and are capable of dealing with the change in our lifestyles. Whole life insurance policies are generally not a good investment. This will give us less stress and more peace.

We must make sure that we have health insurance coverage for all family members. Hospitals and other medical services are getting very expensive for most people. One major operation or a few days' stay in the hospital can cost a substantial amount of money. In addition to the above insurance, we must also have mortgage insurance, automobile insurance, and other hazard insurance.

Investing in Stocks and Annuities

A stock market is a public forum for the trading of the listed public company's stock at an agreed price. The stocks are listed and traded on various stock exchanges—NYSE, NASDAQ, AMEX, or OTC—that specialize in listing stocks of companies in different industries. The largest stock exchange in the world is the New York Stock Exchange (NYSE). It lists the stocks of larger companies, while the NASDAQ lists technology stocks. There are similar stock exchanges in all major countries.

The stock market is one of the most important sources for companies to raise capital by selling shares in the company or by selling bonds. Stock represents ownership (equity) in the company, and bonds represent creditors (debt) of the company. The liquidity that an exchange offers to the investors to quickly buy and sell stock is an added advantage to investors. The stock market is a good measure of a country's economic condition. If the stock market is rising steadily, the country is considered to have an upcoming economy with a stable outlook. Positive growth in the stock market is known as a bull market, and a falling market is known as a bear market.

Most of us invest in stocks as part of our retirement plans or wealth-building plans. The fluctuation in the statistics of NASDAQ (National Association of Securities Dealers Automated Quotations), NYSE, AMEX, or OTC is an indication of stock growth and volatility of the stock investment. Each individual stock can be volatile, stable, or steadily growing.

We must be very careful in trading stocks, especially during these volatile economic times in the US and the world. Annuities take care of some volatility, since they are insurance products and have fixed or variable rates. We pay a cost for management of the annuity funds. They are bought from insurance companies and not from mutual fund companies. If we want to be conservative, we can put money in guaranteed annuity funds or regular annuity funds.

These guaranteed annuities are usually paid as retirement income. You can draw the income on a monthly, quarterly, or annual basis. We can leave all the monies except mandatory drawings; the income will be added to the principal and can be set aside for our spouses or the next generation. Annuity is good for those who cannot control their personal expenditures. This will also provide us with guaranteed income as long as we live. Annuity funds and guaranteed annuity funds absorb the volatility of individual stock markets. Annuities are managed by financial experts, and funds are deposited in various stocks to balance the volatility.

Listed below are a few samples of DJIA (Dow Jones Industrial Average) indexes that illustrate the growth and volatility of major industrial stocks listed on the stock market.

January	1972	1,121
January	2000	11,722
October	2007	14,270
October	2012	13,333
May	2013	15,349

These numbers are based on the performance of all major stocks listed on this stock exchange. However, each individual stock's performance can vary substantially for each corporation. Some stocks grew consistently, and other stocks lost value depending on the performance of the individual company. We experienced these kinds of significant variations for high-tech companies at the beginning of twenty-first century (the dotcom burst). Many people made a lot of money or lost substantial amounts due to the unpredictable volatility.

Stock prices are generally based on the performance of the company. The prices of shares, however, vary based on supply and demand of each individual stock. Stock price variances are affected by many factors and cannot be controlled by individual investors. It becomes cumbersome to keep track of multiple stocks to balance the risks and rewards. For long-term investments, it is better to invest in mutual or annuity funds, which are overseen by knowledgeable investment committees. It is important to choose long-term funds that match your risk tolerance and time horizon.

If we are buying individual stocks, it is better to invest in companies with good returns on investment and sales and that pay good dividends. Lately, due to the global nature of many businesses, outsourcing, and volatile economic conditions, many companies are doing well or poorly due to circumstances beyond their control. Some of them lost value due to competition or not keeping up with the significant technological advancements of the twenty-first century. Some of them lost value due to global competition.

When the stock market crashed in 1929, the value of stocks went down by 89 percent. More than 23,000 people committed suicide, and more than twenty major companies went bankrupt (Friedman, Milton "Monetary History of the United States"). During the crash of 2000, German billionaire Adolph Merckie committed suicide under a train. Rene-Thierry Magon De La Villehuchet lost $1.4 billion by investing in Bernie Madoff's Ponzi scheme. He committed suicide by taking sleeping pills and slitting his wrists. Overall, seventy-two senior executives committed suicide because of the stock market crash in 2007. This also gives us a moral imperative that the stock market can create stress at any time for anyone (Wall Street Journal and New York Daily News).

Please consult a reputable certified financial planner or management company to find investments that suit your needs. We must realize that even expert investors are not always able to keep up with the volatile nature of the stock market. It may be safer than doing it ourselves, but there is no guarantee that any investment will grow consistently.

When we are closer to retirement age, we must put more of our money in safer and more stable investments with more predictable returns and less risk. A basic guideline is to diversify your investments based on age. For example, at the age of sixty, you must invest less than 40 percent in stocks, and at the age of seventy, you must invest less than 30 percent in stocks. The remainder of the investment must be in the form of liquid cash or stable funds with quick access.

We may lose some return on high-growth stocks, but we will minimize losses. As we get older, a steady income is less stressful than worrying about volatile stock market performance. We obtain more peace from stable investments than more unpredictable investments. We all must understand that there are many external factors that affect the value of our investments, and no one can predict the outcome with certainty.

Stress and Peace in Health

Health affects our lives and can create stress or peace depending on the situation. When we are born, we have our own unique characteristics, including some that are genetically transferred from our ancestors. Our basic characteristics are built into our little bodies. Through proper nutrition and care, we grow normally through our teenage years. By this time, we are physically normal people with proportionate body structures.

We need to emphasize that there are many children born without normal bodies or intelligence levels. We do not understand why this happens. We continuously research to find out why these abnormalities happen. We have found few remedies to correct some of the abnormalities through proper planned prenatal care and medical treatments.

We are challenged every day by new abnormalities and continue researching to find remedies for them. The priority of our research is based on the seriousness of the diseases. Reasons for these abnormalities are beyond most people's comprehension and are a major stress factor for those affected by them. The country and medical research facilities are financially stressed from trying to research every abnormality.

We understand that by the late teens, a normal body is formed with proper nutrition. It is essential that we continue proper behavior and ingest proper nutrients as the basis for normal lives. As previously discussed, everyone was created uniquely with his or her own basic characteristics and physical appearance. It is our choice to maintain, improve, or destroy this uniqueness.

We are given freedom by our Creator to choose our actions to change ourselves. We must know, however, that we do not have control over our births, basic characteristics, or deaths. We need to continuously monitor our health and engage in proper exercise. There is no guarantee that proper behavior and pre-testing will alleviate all problems. If we can detect problems at an early stage and take corrective actions to alleviate them, we can forestall problems in the future. These actions will alleviate a lot of stress and give us more peaceful lives.

We need to insure that we live properly to preserve our physical, mental, and spiritual growth to the best of our abilities. Since everyone is unique, there are no standard procedures for our behaviors. There are, however, some general guidelines we can apply to our physical conditions. For example, as a general guideline, a person's waist size should not be more than half of his or her height. A person who is six feet tall should have a waist that measures no more than thirty-six inches. Physical appearance varies from person to person and is based on his or her unique situation, race, sex, and cultural background.

Doctors should be integral parts of our health teams. A proper blood test reference range chart can identify some deviations from normal health guidelines. The higher the deviation from the normal guidelines, the greater the chances of higher abnormalities and this will create more unhealthy situations and higher stress. Medical experts can interpret symptoms properly and treat us to rectify the problems.

We must make sure that we start getting these tests and information when we are young to avoid aggravating the symptoms and creating more unhealthy conditions. Corrective treatment at an early age will help a person make the right choices and give him or her better long-term health and peace. There are no guarantees that all these tests will alleviate all the problems. There are always exceptions to general rules.

When we are young, we may not feel it is necessary to have various health tests. The earlier we detect health problems, the earlier we can take corrective actions and avoid unnecessary stress. Preventive health care is always better than facing emergency medical situations.

We must also understand that excessive abuses of any kind can be major factors in creating serious abnormalities and ill health. Excessive consumption of alcohol can have an adverse effect and cause cardiovascular disease, chronic liver disease, cancer, and damage to the nervous system. Excessive smoking can cause lung cancer, respiratory problems, coronary disease, stroke, heart disease, narrowing blood vessels, leukemia, and stomach cancer.

These types of problems can create major financial stress for our families and people close to us and can adversely affect our peace. Excessive abnormal behaviors can cause sicknesses; these illnesses not only affect us and our families, but also the people we associate with. We must understand that our lives are not only for us, but also to share with others. We must always avoid abusive behaviors that can make us unhealthy and cause financial and physical stress for us and other people involved in our lives. We must understand that only we can be responsible for our actions.

As you may know, medical expenses in the US have grown twice as fast as the consumer price index since 1980. Health costs were about 18 percent of GNP in 1980 and rose to 25 percent in 1992. Health costs per capita in the US are the highest in the world. Our cost in 2008 was $7,500 per capita, as compared to Canada's $4,100, UK's $3,100, and Japan's $2,700.[6]

This is a major drain on our national economic resources and creates significant stress for everyone, including employers. We must try to do our best so that we can keep ourselves healthy, alleviate major stress, and enjoy more peace.

It is essential that we all do our share of health maintenance to reduce the increasing national health care costs. If we all have good preventive medical care, we can reduce total health costs significantly. Health costs continue to grow day by day and have become a major financial and political issue. We must reduce runaway medical costs by offering better preventive medical care and reducing the corruption and legal costs in this industry.

A combined effort by everyone involved—patients, doctors, and health providers—can improve the efficiency of the health care system. We all must closely watch Medicare and Medicaid spending to help the government eliminate abuses within the system. Patients and doctors must not request unnecessary tests and treatments. We must expose the abuses in the medical charges and payment system. We must discourage frivolous lawsuits. We need tort reform for medical insurance and legal claims.

When integrity and honesty are present in the health care system, we will be able to reduce health care costs while increasing our personal health. These actions will result in an efficient system that will reduce stress for all the participants in the system.

Obesity

There are many health concerns. Since the end of World War II, obesity has become an ever-growing problem. It has caused increasing health and financial stress. Most obesity can be controlled if we understand how to manage it. Obesity is defined by the World Health Organization as abnormal or excessive fat accumulation that represents a risk to an individual's health. Eighty percent of obese people have type II diabetes. (LSU Health Science Center, Genetics and Louisiana Families).

The major problem of obesity is that the body is not able to produce enough insulin. Obesity can cause many health problems, such as coronary heart disease, type two diabetes, cancer, hypertension, high cholesterol, liver and gall bladder disease, sleep apnea, respiratory problems, osteoarthritis, abnormal menses, infertility, and other disorders.[7]

Obesity can be measured by body mass index (BMI), which is calculated by the following formula:

(Weight in pounds x 703) / (height in inches x height in inches)

A body mass index of 18.5–24.9 is normal, 25–29 is overweight, and over 30 is obese.

According to the World Health Organization, obesity is a global problem. There are 1.6 billion adults who are overweight, and over 400 million children under the age of twenty are obese.

The major causes of obesity are high-fat, nutrient-poor foods and a lack of exercise. Our obesity problem continues to grow and has become a major national health problem. In 2009, obesity-related health care costs were over $190 billion in the US (Centers for Disease Control and Prevention). Obesity-related health issues require costly, long-term medical care and regimens.

Obesity is a disorder that can be controlled in a majority of cases. Consumption of fewer calories and regular exercise can help control obesity.

Parents must play a lead role to insure that children eat healthy food. When we do this from an early age, it becomes a lifelong habit to eat healthy food. Many times, parents are busy working and do not find time to cook at home. Fast food is an all-too-common alternative from a very early age. This bad eating habit becomes ingrained in children, resulting in obesity.

In addition, we must help children lose weight through proper diet and exercise. Most of us consume more food than we need. In order to avoid this, we must start serving in smaller portions similar to the ones of the 1960s and 1970s. This can be accomplished by eating on small plates or by controlling portions of food.

In addition, technological advancements and the Internet can be detrimental to children's social activities and physical exercise. Children spend too much time watching television and on the Internet, resulting in less physical activity.

We are losing personal contact, resulting in further deterioration of our mental and physical health. We must make sure that children have enough physical exercise and participate in sports on a regular basis. This must be a part of the school curriculum. Even during summer holidays, they must be physically active.

It is essential that employers and schools work to reduce obesity through wellness and incentive programs. Simple exercises, like walking, do not cost money. We must try to walk at least two to five miles a day. This will keep us healthier and thinner.

We, as individuals, must keep ourselves healthy to alleviate physical and financial stress due to poor health and the associated monetary and mental costs. This will result in less stress and more peace of mind.

Stress during Natural Disasters

A natural disaster is a major adverse event resulting from the earth's natural hazards and has a significant effect on human populations. We have discussed some of the items we can try to control by our own actions. Sometimes we have to face challenges beyond our control. These are natural disasters, such as earthquakes, hurricanes, tornados, fires, floods, ice storms, dust storms, volcanic eruptions, tsunamis, landslides etc. which can happen anywhere at any time.

Some of us face major natural disasters that can alter our lifestyles. In the event we are fortunate enough to not face those events directly, we will come across people who experienced the serious consequences of natural disasters. The adverse effects of such disasters will create serious financial and emotional stress in our lives. As mentioned earlier, we should always be prepared for the unexpected. This will help us to face the consequences of natural disasters better.

Most of us, however, are not prepared to face natural disasters without any stress. When we face major disasters, we understand that we have little control over our lives. During such events, we can lose many valuable memories. We could even lose our dear ones, which would cause emotional stress for the rest of our lives.

Natural disasters have killed many people. Listed below are some major disasters since the 1920s. There were many other disasters prior to this period.

Year	Description	Deaths
1931	China Flood	430,000
1976	Tangshan Earthquake	780,000
1970	Bangladesh Cyclone	500,000
2004	Indonesia Tsunami	300,000
1920	China Earthquake	230,000
1923	Japan Earthquake	142,000
2008	Burma Cyclone	138,000
1991	Bangladesh Cyclone	123,000
1908	Italy Earthquake	123,000
1948	Turkmenistan Earthquake	110,000

In addition, there are many diseases and epidemics that cause numerous deaths. Some of them are controllable, whereas others are unpredictable. It is essential that we act morally to avoid getting or giving communicable diseases. If we love others the way we love God and ourselves, we will be able to live with good moral strength. This will reduce our stress and increase our peace.

Listed below are some major diseases and their death tolls.

Diseases	Est. Deaths	Comments
Smallpox	300 million Worldwide	eradicated in 1980
Measles	200 million Worldwide	150 years
Black Plague	100 million in Asia, Europe, and Africa	1300-1720
Malaria	80-100 million Worldwide	20th century
Spanish Flu	50-100 million Worldwide	1918-1920

Tuberculosis	40-100 million Worldwide	20th century
AIDS	30 million Worldwide	1981-present
Asia Flu	4 million Worldwide	1956-1958
Influenza	250,000 Worldwide	2009-present

In addition, there are many kinds of fires, like camp fires, lightning fires, and forest fires. We have had numerous fires in the US during the last ten years (National Fire Protection Association). Many properties were destroyed or damaged. Ice storms in Quebec in 1998 caused thirty deaths and extensive power outages.

Many people experienced loss of homes, family members and property as well as financial loss. These natural disasters uprooted and separated many families. Many people lost their businesses and jobs. In addition, families suffer from stress created by financial and emotional losses. These natural disasters cost us billions of dollars for reconstruction and redevelopment. Some people are not able to rebuild their homes. These are some of the natural disasters we have no control over.

These are difficult times, and most of us are not prepared physically, financially, or mentally to face these uncertainties. We are very seldom prepared to overcome these incidents and experience major stress when we encounter these natural disasters. In addition to the uncontrollable natural disasters, we face other disasters, such as plane crashes, shipwrecks, shooting deaths, and automobile accidents, which can create stress on a daily basis.

That is why it is important to keep our houses in order by prudently managing factors that we can control. If we do not have the controllable factors under control, it will be more difficult for us to face uncontrollable, external adversities. When our finances and family lives are in order, we can face these adversities better and reduce our stress substantially. When we are better prepared to face the controllable factors, we can be more at peace. These natural disasters can happen to any one of us at any time. Disasters make us understand that we do not have as much control over our lives as we would like. We must enjoy life with what we have and be grateful to our Creator.

Stress during Personal Attack

There are major conflicts going on in the world due to many factors. A continuous fight between good and evil has been going on since time began. Usually, conflicts happen when there are not enough resources to go around.

Even though there may be enough resources for everyone, they cannot be distributed properly because of the world's geography, physical layout, and personal or political conflicts. This resource distribution can be applied to money, power, sexual needs, religious freedom, and people's perception of right or wrong. We have conflicts between rich and poor, rulers and their subjects, dictators and the ruled, nations, religious denominations, and races, to mention a few.

We read about these conflicts in newspapers, on the Internet, and on television. Sometimes we wish that we were not part of them. We could, however, be involved in these conflicts either directly or indirectly. Ethnic cleansing and racial fights are common all around the world. Everyone wants peaceful coexistence, but we are not prepared to tolerate and accommodate other people's needs, resulting in major conflicts. In other words, we want peaceful coexistence but only on our terms.

There are massive persecutions throughout the world due to conflicts of race, power struggles, ideological differences, and abuses of power.

Some of these major genocides and persecutions throughout the world are listed below. Many people were killed due to these atrocities.

In the 1890s, King Leopold II of Belgium killed more than 8 million people. In the 1930s and 1940s, Adolph Hitler killed more than 20 million people in Europe. In the 1940s, Josef Stalin of Russia killed more than 10 million people. Japan's Hideki Tojo killed more than 5 million people in the 1940s during World War II. In the 1960s in China, Mao Zedong killed more than 50 million people.

There were numerous other genocides in the world. Pol Pot of Cambodia killed 1.7 million people in the 1970s. Saddham Hussein of Iran killed more than six hundred thousand people in the 1980s. Mullah Omar (the Taliban) of Afghanistan killed more than four hundred thousand people in the 1970s. During the twentieth century, genocides accounted for over 105 million deaths (Reported by Genocide Watch with International Alliance to Educate Genocides).

We are fortunate that we live in the US, where there are no major ethnic cleansing problems. We had a major disaster on September 11, 2001 when terrorists attacked the World Trade Center in New York with our own airplanes. More than three thousand innocent people lost their lives in this attack. We all may face such situations. This kind of inhuman act can happen to anyone, at any time, anywhere.

These are the reasons why it is essential for all of us to keep our controllable factors in balance and in proper order. We must all be prepared to face these kinds of situations without major, long-term stress. We must always control our lives to the best of our abilities so that when we are faced with uncontrollable events, we can lead our lives with less stress. It does not matter how prepared we are; these kinds of unpredictable, inhuman acts create stress and a lack of peace in our lives.

We can reduce major conflicts by tolerating and accommodating other people's ideologies. As human beings, we are all imperfect, and we must learn to forgive, forget, and tolerate other people's behaviors. We can only do our portions. The people who are instrumental in creating these major conflicts and destruction serve their needs. They are not concerned about the victims in their inhuman acts. We have seen in many cases that these cruel leaders suffered at the end, committing suicide or being murdered mercilessly.

As previously mentioned, if we lead proper lives and do not abuse ourselves physically, mentally, or spiritually, we build our own personal strength, which will assist us in facing most adverse conditions without major stress. Despite adverse conditions, we will learn how to live in peace with pure love and hope.

Stress and Peace in Old Age and Life after Retirement

We all age due to DNA (deoxyribonucleic acid) wear and tear. DNA contains the genetic instructions used in the development of all living organisms and viruses. Daily we reproduce billions of new cells. This is similar to photocopying the original repeatedly. As time goes by, we cannot produce the quantity and quality of cells we need. In addition, the cells produced are not always exact copies of the originals. This results in deterioration of both quantity and quality of cells, which results in the aging process.

There is no universal acceptance of old age. The rules regarding what constitutes old age continue to fluctuate as lifespans increase. The retirement age is generally considered to be the beginning of old age. After retirement, we start missing our work, coworkers, and social interactions.

Generally, older people develop different lifestyles, engage in different work, or do not work at all. Older people show wrinkles, gray hair, hair loss, hearing loss, eyesight deterioration, dementia, reduced reflexes, increased need for medical care, etc.

Aging also depends on the general health condition of the individual and varies from person to person. The Berlin Aging Study defines old age as between seventy and 103 (Berlin Aging Study). Old age, also called *senescence* in human beings, is the final stage a normal lifespan.

For older people to stay healthy, they must be sure to eat nutritious food. They need regular medical checkups to detect health problems earlier and take corrective actions. Excessive eating or use of alcohol and drugs are not solutions for loneliness or ill health. Regular, consistent exercise is necessary for muscle tone and flexibility. It is important for the elderly to develop activities, such as reading, writing, or doing volunteer work, to keep them busy. Doing volunteer work is very fulfilling and betters the community. There are many organizations and charities that desperately need volunteer help.

Many older people live alone or with spouses. There are many people over seventy-five who live alone after losing their spouses. In 2009, 25 percent of men and 49 percent of women over seventy-five lived alone (Department of Health and Human Services USA). Just because they are living alone does not necessarily mean they are lonely. Many of them are socially and physically active.

Old-age problems, such as ill health, lack of social contacts, loneliness, and depression, vary. The more relationships, hobbies, and social contacts they have, the less they will experience loneliness and depression. Ill health, such as sight, hearing, and physical incapacities, will make people feel older and lonely. These lonely feelings can cause depression and deterioration of one's health.

Being disabled is no excuse for not exercising. There are many facilities and types of exercises tailored for people with disabilities. The elderly need to contact people or organizations that specialize in assisting older people with disabilities.

They should never feel that because they are older and disabled, they are beyond help. Attending church, temple, etc. is helpful for attaining peace and fellowship. There are a variety of services offered for the elderly by these organizations. They should take advantage of these services and maintain social relationships. By staying engaged socially and physically, the elderly can lead healthier and happier lives with decreased stress.

Having good relationships and interactions with their children and grandchildren will help them alleviate loneliness and depression. Be sure to visit your children frequently, and invite them to be part of your social life. To accomplish this requires making adjustments to their schedules and priorities.

If the elderly do not make adjustments to accommodate other people, they will not be able to effectively interact socially. The less interaction they have, the lonelier they become. They may feel isolated, depressed, and stressed. Making time for others is important to reduce stress and for peace of mind.

For older people to stay healthy, they must be sure to eat nutritious food. They need regular medical checkups to detect health problems earlier and take corrective actions. Excessive eating or use of alcohol and drugs are not solutions for loneliness or ill health. Regular, consistent exercise is necessary for muscle tone and flexibility.

It is important for the elderly to develop activities, such as reading, writing, or doing volunteer work, to keep them busy. Doing volunteer work is very fulfilling and betters the community. There are many organizations and charities that desperately need volunteer help.

Many older people live alone or with spouses. There are many people over seventy-five who live alone after losing their spouses. In 2009, 25 percent of men and 49 percent of women over seventy-five lived alone

(Department of Health and Human Services USA). Just because they are living alone does not necessarily mean they are lonely. Many of them are socially and physically active.

Currently, there are many anti-aging therapies and discoveries that can extend one's lifespan. We are experimenting with repairing or replacing DNA. The more proficient we become in this area, the more we can extend our lifespans. We can expect life expectancy to grow to 120 years for future generations.

Increases in the older population as a percent of total population will increase the national burden of health care, pensions, and Social Security benefits. This will be a major challenge for individuals, corporations, and the government. More than half the baby boomers in America are going to see their hundredth birthdays and beyond in excellent health.

Life expectancy has increased due to many positive factors, such as better health care, increased health awareness, and social and physical activities for older generations. In 1900, the older generation numbered 3 million (4 percent) out of 76 million, and in 2000, the number grew to 35 million (12 percent) out of 280 million. We expect the older population to grow to 65 million by 2020 (16 percent) out of 395 million (U.S. Census Bureau). "We are looking at the life spans for the baby boomers. The life span of generations after baby boomers may be from 120–150 years of age" (Dr. Ronald Klatz "Research on Basic of Healthy Living).

The increases in the older population as a percent of total population will increase the national burden of health care, pensions, and Social Security benefits. This will be a major challenge for individuals, corporations, and the government. More than half the baby boomers in America are going to see their hundredth birthdays and beyond in excellent health.

This may result in major reductions in medical benefits, Social Security, and other pension benefits in future, greatly affecting the elderly. These are the reasons why we should be more prudent in setting aside enough funds for retirement needs. If we do not do it properly, we will face serious shortages of resources and will create major stress during our old age. Most people at this age have grandchildren and great- grandchildren.

For many people, it is very difficult to adjust to retirement. This is generally applicable to the people who spent most of their time between work, home, and family. They become empty-nesters with no one except their spouses. Prior to their retirement, they filled their time with work and job-related social involvement. They might find it hard to fill their time with only their spouses. If they are not prepared it can create conflict in their lives.

Some people look forward to life after retirement. They have set aside enough resources to travel and visit places they did not have time to visit when working. They take long vacations and visit interesting locations. They can take time to visit families and relations and participate in some of the recreation they were interested in but did not have time for while working.

The Social Security Act of 1935 was adopted to relieve the hardships caused by the Great Depression for the elderly who were granted Social Security pensions. The full eligibility of Social Security was determined as sixty-five. Lately, however, the full benefit age has been changed based on date of birth. In addition people who are eligible can also get some Medicaid help. This is good supplementary income for retirees. Socially security income along with other saving you made, while working, must suffice for a good living for most of the people.

During old age, being physically limited can allow the elderly to spend more time with their family and friends. If there is no family near or the family is not able to have an elderly relative with them, an assisted living facility is a good choice. Having social interactions with the other residents will reduce stress and increase peacefulness.

Stress and Peace in Hobbies

A hobby is a regular activity or interest that is undertaken for pleasure, typically during one's leisure time. A hobby can also be a regular activity or interest that is undertaken for pleasure with or without any pay. This is an opportunity for us to pursue our passions and interests and indulge in activities that could not be done while we work. Most people spend their time reading, watching television or working on computers. They feel bored, because they don't feel like they are doing anything useful. They spend too much time sitting around, complaining about boredom and stress.

Most people spend their lives working for companies or their own businesses and spend the remainder of the time with family and doing social activities. Most of them do not spend time and resources to develop hobbies prior to retirement to alleviate after-retirement shock.

Hobbies and social activities can make them happier and healthier people. Hobbies are a great way to reduce stress and can be developed at any age. Everyone should try attempting new things until he or she finds endeavors that he or she enjoys. This might create some stress at the beginning. However, those who pursue hobbies will become fascinated by these new interests, thus relieving the initial stress. It is essential for every one of us to develop hobbies that enable us to expand our horizons while gaining enlightenment outside day-to-day living.

There are some fortunate people whose passions become their hobbies, and the hobby becomes the person's career. There are athletes who play basketball, baseball, football, golf, tennis, hockey, or other sports who are talented enough to turn their hobbies into well-paid careers. These people get to enjoy their hobbies and live very nice lives. This is an ideal situation and is only achieved by a very few people. Most of us, however, are not fortunate enough to develop hobbies into careers.

Hobbies can be anything a person always wanted to do but did not have enough time and resources for while he or she worked. It is essential that people develop their own hobbies or ask for guidance from others to develop hobbies. There are many community centers, YMCAs, religious and social organizations that are willing and able to assist hobby-seekers in their needs.

People can try a number of hobbies that interest them and select the most enjoyable hobby to keep them busy after retirement. They have plenty of time after retirement to stay busy and avoid boredom. Hobbies can be physical, such as sports and games, or mental, such as reading, knitting, painting, playing cards, or writing. One of the major problems most retirees face is that they do not know what to do with their after-work time. These hobbies will definitely help them fill the time and derive some enjoyment. This will help them to keep healthy and be more at peace.

Listed below are a few hobbies that people can pursue to keep them active and reduce stress and ill health.

Start learning and playing chess or cards, focusing on improving concentration. People can spend more time reading books that will connect them with great thinkers and writers and improve their knowledge in many areas.

Learn to play a musical instrument that can also be used for social events. Dancing is great for cardiovascular exercise and is a good way to meet new people.

Woodworking is another hobby that can be used for making presents for family members and friends. If woodworking is too expensive, start whittling pieces of wood.

Gardening is a great hobby for those who want to connect with nature and get fresh air. Gardeners can also grow some food for them and give gifts to others.

They can play physical sports, such as baseball, bowling, and golf. Increases in sports activities will also make them healthier as long as they don't overdo it. Car restoration is an exciting hobby and can increase mechanical skills.

There are many additional hobbies that will help occupy a retired person's leisure time, such as metalworking, hunting, marksmanship, collecting unusual items, camping, hiking, fishing, model building, leather working, and archery, to name a few. They can pretty well start any hobby depending on their interests, passions, and the time and resources available.

They can do volunteer services and help others in hospitals, retirement homes, religious institutions, homeless shelters, etc. They may be able to help food pantries and food kitchens to serve the needy.

A person can volunteer as a consultant based on his or her education and experience. There are many people who need help starting their own businesses or young people seeking mentors. This will give them purpose and also can establish social interactions with other volunteers and staff members.

Hobbies can also help fill in their time and establish new social interactions. If people have no purpose, it can lead to loneliness. Loneliness is a feeling of emptiness and distress and can create inadequate social relationships. Loneliness and isolation can cause anger, resentment, and a lack of sleep. It can lead to destructive habits, such as alcoholism, smoking, drug addiction, etc. This will result in serious diseases, such as cancer, stroke, cardiovascular diseases, hypertension, etc.

Hobbies can help balance life. This will provide an outlet to create something personally fulfilling and enjoyable. Hobbies can reduce trials and tribulations. They can assist in meeting and handling challenges more easily. Hobbies give people an opportunity to make things for those who are special to them. Hobbies are helpful in improving health and social activities. Those who partake in hobbies feel better and feel less stress and more peace.

Peace from Sharing Our God-Given Talents, Time, and Resources

Webster Dictionary defines talent as "any natural ability and power." Talent results in consistently recurring patterns of thought and behavior. Talent cannot be subordinated by knowledge and behavior, because it is consistent and enduring. For example, public speaking and music are good examples of talents. Talent can be improved with more knowledge and experience. Knowledge and experience-based skills can be changed easily, unlike talent-based skills.

Time is a dimension in which events can be ordered from the past through the present into the future. Time is also the duration of events and the intervals between them. Time is what a clock measures and what keeps everything from happening at once. Time is part of the fundamental structure of the universe. Time is a dimension, independent of events in which events occur in sequence. Our time on earth is limited, so it is essential that we use it wisely and prudently. Once our time has elapsed, we cannot retrieve it. In addition, time waits for no one. We can never extend our lifetimes or buy more time with our money or any other resources.

Resources are economic or productive factors required to accomplish an activity or as a means to undertake an enterprise and arrive at the desired results. The most important resources are land, labor, material, and capital. Other resources include energy, infrastructure, information, entrepreneurship, and expertise in management, to name a few.

First of all, we all have to understand that we are created by God with a purpose in life. Every one of us is created with a different set of talents and purpose, and no one is superior to anyone else. Everyone does different tasks and has a different set of talents and passions to perform these with. Everyone has a unique lifetime and resource. Do not try to imitate others, because your purpose is different from theirs. You must be content with what you are; this contentment will make you joyful and peaceful and enables you to live with less stress.

When we pool our talents, time, and resources properly, the world will be a better place to live in. If we do not complement each other's needs, we all will live in stress and with little peace. Together, we can accomplish the total purpose of God Almighty and live in peace.

"I am the wine, you are the branches. If a man remains in me and me in him, he will bear much fruit. Apart from me, you can do nothing" (John 15:5 NIV).

Our accomplishments are very important, but helping others and living a peaceful life is the most significant goal in life. If we are greedy and selfish and consume too many resources without sharing with others, we will end our lives in loneliness and without peace of mind.

We must understand that we as individuals do not have total control of our life journeys. If we look into the rearview mirrors of our lives, we can see that our life journeys did not unfold as we planned. Many of our plans did not materialize. Many materialized plans were not ours. Many things happen in our lives that put us on a path never known to us. God gives us freedom to choose our actions and makes us responsible for the outcomes. Even so, we do not understand the complete plans and purposes of our life journeys.

There are sufficient talents and resources to make sure that the needs of the human race are met. However, due to some people's unwillingness to share, we can never meet everybody's needs. Mahatma Gandhi told us that "we have enough resources in this world for every one's need but not for everyone's greed."

Many people suffer because of the greed. Let us share our talents and resources as needed to make this world a peaceful place to live for all of us. We all know that as individuals, we cannot solve all the problems in the world. If we can make a difference in people's lives and make at least one person smile every day, we will see a better world. The world will be a harmonious place that is filled with joy and peace.

We have been given our talents and resources not only for our use, but also to supplement other people's needs. We are allowed to enjoy life with our resources, but it is not fair for us to consume all our resources only for our own enjoyment. This is a selfish lifestyle, and we will soon realize that sharing makes us happier than consumption.

We can help other people financially, provide companionship, visit them, pray for them when they are ill, help the needy, give shelter, provide clothes, visit them in hospital, visit them in prison, etc. We can also assist them by doing things for them that they cannot do for themselves.

> And do not forget to do well and to share with others, for with such sacrifices God is pleased. (Hebrews 13:15 NIV)

Our lives are God's gift to us. How we live is our gift to God. Our stewardship of time and resources does not mean that we have to keep busy all the time. We must make sure that God is always with us.

So we say with confidence, The Lord is my helper; I will not be afraid. What can mere man do to me? (Hebrews 13:6 NIV)

Come to me, all you who labor and are heavy laden, and I will give you rest. (Matthew 11:28 NIV)

Time spent in prayer and nurturing good relationships with our family and friends is time well spent. The time we spend socializing and enjoying sports, nature, and the world around us is time well spent. Our time and resources can be spent with friends, establishing better relationships. Attending religious services and establishing fellowship is time well spent.

There is a misconception that the time we spend always means personal rewards and additional earnings for us. We can be productive and resourceful by just helping the needy will make our lives less stressful and give us more peace.

Peace from Love

We always search for peace and joy in our lives. It will be easy to achieve peace and joy when we start loving the people we associate with. We must follow God. God is love, and we must practice love to make our lives more meaningful and peaceful. Once we practice true love, we will find that our lives will have very little stress and more peace.

> Jesus replied to them love the Lord your God with all your heart, with all your soul and with all your mind. This is first and greatest commandment. And the second is like it: Love thy neighbor as yourself. (Matthew 22:37-39 NIV)

> Though the mountains be shaken and the hills removed, yet my unfailing love for you will not be shaken nor my covenant of peace be removed. (Isaiah 54:10 NIV)

We know that Christ's love for us is unquestionable. He came to the world, lived with us, and died for our sins. We lose our joy and peace when we do not share our love with others. We lose respect for our parents, because we do not practice true love. Our divorce rate is too high, because we fail to love each other, especially during difficult times.

We have numerous conflicts in our lives, because we do not practice true love. If we love one another, God will always be with us. If we do not have true love, it will lead us to loneliness, anxiety, helplessness, loss of self-esteem, and even insanity. Let us all practice true love and make our lives peaceful.

In order to alleviate stress and obtain peace, we must learn how to practice true love. We may not be able to accomplish all aspects of love completely. However, when we start practicing love, we will find a difference in our behavior with other people and have more enjoyment, which will lead to contented lives.

> Love is patient, love is kind, it does not envy, it does not boast, it is not proud, it is not rude, it is not self-seeking, it is not easily angered, it keeps no record of wrongs, it does not delight in evil, but love rejoices with truth, it always protects, always trusts, always hopes, always perseveres, love never fails. (1 Corinthians 13:4–8 NIV)

Love Is Patient

In trying circumstances, the patient person will be enduring, even-tempered, tolerant, understanding, and diligent. We cannot control everything, and a patient person understands this well and does not overreact to circumstances beyond his or her control. When we are patient, we can be more productive and less stressed.

Love Is Kind

Kind people are good, benevolent, considerate, helpful, humane, compassionate, gentle, loving, and affectionate. We should be kind to all the people we come in contact with.

Love Does Not Envy

Envy is defined as resentment that occurs when a person lacks another's perceived qualities, achievements, or possessions and wishes that he or she had all those qualities. We read in the bible that Cain slew Abel because of envy. Envy is a cause for much conflict, unhappiness, and sickness in the world. Envy creates a lot of stress and a lack of peace. "Envy is one of the most potent causes of unhappiness" (Bertrand Russell).

Love Does Not Boast

People boast or brag by making exaggerated statements about themselves using deception and excessive pride. People must never boast about their possessions, because people who boast show a lack of self-worth. It also makes other people uncomfortable. People who boast define themselves only by their possessions. We must learn how to appreciate others rather than boasting.

Love Is Not Proud

Pride is defined as inflated ego and disdain for what one considers inferior. We must understand that everybody has different talents. We all need to complement each other rather than compete with each other. Together, we can accomplish anything, and we must treat others as a part of the team.

Love Is Not Rude

Rudeness is defined as primitiveness, ignorance, unlearnedness, incivility, savageness, coarseness, or vulgarity. You must always treat others as you want to be treated.

Love Is Not Self-Seeking

Self-seeking people promote themselves and their interests even at other people's expense. They are selfish and promote their own agendas rather than considering the needs of others.

Love Is Not Easily Angered

Anger is an emotion related to a psychological interpretation of having been offended, overpowered, wronged, or denied and a tendency to react through retaliation. We can apply pressure to control anger for a short period, but it will explode in due course unless we learn to control it.

Love Does Not Keep Any Record of Wrongdoing

Love is forgiving and does not hold grudges against another person. We must see the goodness in others, not faults. We must always understand that none of us is perfect and that we all make mistakes.

Love Does Not Delight in Evil

Delight is a feeling of extreme gratification aroused by something good or desired. Evil is something that is a source of suffering or injury or that results in poverty and injustice. Those who live in evil will always be without peace and happiness.

Love Rejoices with the Truth

Whoever lives by the truth comes into the light. True love is happiness and finding joy in things that are valid, authentic, accurate, and real. Life with truth and integrity makes us strong and unafraid of anything.

Love Always Protects

If you love someone, you will never encourage him or her to do anything against his or her conscience. Love takes the good with bad and protects and tolerates the same.

Love Always Trusts

Trust is confidence given by someone to others with reliability and strength. The one who trusts is willing to rely on the actions of another party or group of people.

Love Always Hopes

Hope is a feeling, expectation, or desire for a certain thing to happen. It is an emotional state of being reasonably confident that positive results will happen. When there is no hope in our lives, we will be desperate and stressed.

Love Always Perseveres

Love is a feeling that will persevere for a long time and protect from harm or injury.

Love Never Fails

Love will always make the desirable or intended objective and never let us fail.

> I have a faith that can move mountains but have not love, I am nothing. And now these three remains, faith, hope and love. But the greatest of these is love. (1 Corinthians 13:13 NIV)

> For God so loved the world that He gave his one and only Son, that whoever believes in Him shall not perish, but have eternal life. (John 3:16 NIV)

In Buddhism, *karuna* is compassion and mercy that reduces the suffering of others. Love is unconditional, requires considerable self-acceptance, and refers to detachment from materialistic possession and unselfish interest in other's welfare.

Islam teaches us that God does not love those who overstep boundaries, those who spread corruption, unbelievers, wrongdoers, oppressors, the wasteful, the proud, the boastful, the treacherous, or those who are given to crime and evil speaking.

In Hinduism, love is a sacrament that one gives selflessly. The one who gives does not expect anything in return.

In Hebrew, *ahava* is the most commonly used term for both interpersonal love and love of God. Love also includes grace, goodwill, kindness, compassion, and affection.

In Sikhism, love means love for the Lord and His creation, truth, contentment, compassion, and humility.

> Love is composed of a single soul inhibiting two bodies. (Aristotle)
>
> I have found the paradox that if you love until it hurts, there can be no more hurt, only more love. Let us always meet each other with smile, for the smile is the beginning of love. (Mother Teresa)
>
> I have decided to stick with love hate is too great a burden to bear. (Dr. Martin Luther King, Jr.)
>
> Where there is love there is life. (Mahatma Gandhi)
>
> The greatest happiness of life is the conviction that we are loved, loved ourselves, or rather loved in spite of ourselves. (Victor Hugo)

Most of our stress and lack of peace are due to not having true love for others in our hearts. Let us take a look at each of the ingredients of love and see whether we can practice love with God's grace. True love never dies, bonds for a lifetime, and lasts forever.

> Evil is the result of what happens when man does not have God's love present in his heart. (Albert Einstein)

Stress and Peace from Expectations and Gratitude

We all live in a world with many expectations. The expectation may be a strong desire for something good to happen or a feeling that something bad may happen. We get bound up by expectations from the day we are born. When we have expectations that are too high, there will be greater disappointments. If we keep expectations in balance, we will find freedom, less stress, and more peace.

Disappointment is the feeling of dissatisfaction that follows the failure of expectations or hopes to be met. There is nothing wrong with expectations for higher-level accomplishments. We become disappointed only when we expect benefits for ourselves from the results. When we do not get the benefits we expect, we will be very disappointed. When our expectations are for another person's betterment, we are usually not as disappointed when the result does not happen. We are less stressed in this situation and come to the belief that the other person will try again to make it happen.

Most of the time, the expectation is unilateral, and the other party is passive. The other party does not even know that we had expectations of his or her performance. This happens when we are closely connected with the other person and imagine his or her actions as our own expectations. This situation is very common; parents have expectations of their children, children of parents, between spouses and in-laws etc. These expectations are based on good intentions but are very emotional and sometimes selfish.

We can alleviate disappointment if the expectations are communicated to the concerned parties. If we do not discuss these expectations in advance, we do not have any right to be disappointed. We can further reduce our disappointments if we come to an agreement between the parties involved. This kind of agreement happens in a formal relationship, such as a teacher-student or employer-employee relationship. We can make the other party accountable by verbal or written agreement. There are always consequences for not complying with the agreement. We can lower expectations to reduce disappointments.

As a general rule, pessimistic people have higher levels of disappointment. Optimistic people are usually more flexible and have a better understanding of the situation. This will result in fewer disappointments. Unfortunately, most disappointments come from not meeting a one-sided emotional expectation.

Expectations lead us to feel disappointments, betrayal, distrust, anger, etc. This will result in people getting sick and experiencing headaches, intestinal difficulties, moist palms, and long-term chronic problems.

There are many ways to handle or reduce disappointment. We must be optimistic and understand that everything we expect in life does not happen. Everything in life's journey is an experience, and we must try to enjoy the moments we get. We must be prepared to experience good and bad things in life and adjust our attitudes to accept both failures and successes.

We can reduce or eliminate our disappointments by communicating with the people involved. We must come to an understanding between both parties to insure that both take corrective actions to reduce disappointment. We can accomplish this by relaxing expectations.

We must never dwell on disappointments. We must redirect our thinking to more positive thoughts. We must realize that we might face many major disappointments in our lives that are beyond our control. We can face major thunderstorms during our planned vacations. We might face major natural disasters, like floods, fires, earthquakes, etc. These affect many people and are of greater consequence than personal disappointments.

We might lose our jobs that we depend on for our livelihoods. We might have chronically ill members of our families who need constant attention and medical care. We might have unexpected deaths in our families. When we consider all these, we will find that our disappointments are not important.

Krishna says in Gita, "Therefore without being attached to the fruits of activities, one should act as a matter of duty for, by working without attachment one attains the Supreme."

Buddhism teaches us that "expectations are like fairy tales and myths, they are alluring but ultimately leave us disillusioned and disappointed, which are the fore bearers of suffering. Today I am really letting it go and it could not have been more liberating."

The Lord declares, "For I know the plans I have for you, plans to prosper you and not harm you, plans to give you hope and future" (Jeremiah 29:11 NIV).

In order for us to experience joyful and peaceful lives, we must help others without any personal expectations or benefits.

Gratitude is a feeling from the heart or attitude in acknowledgement of benefits we receive or will receive from others. It is very important to understand that spirituality is able to increase a person's ability to be more grateful. Most world religions teach gratitude to God.

The Hebrew Scriptures are full of expressions of gratitude. All things came from God, and gratitude is important to followers of Judaism. "O Lord God, I will give thanks to you forever and I will give thanks to the Lord with my whole heart" (Psalm 3:12, 9:1 NIV).

The Koran is filled with the practice of gratitude. Islam encourages its followers to be grateful in all circumstances. Prophet Muhammad said, "Gratitude for the abundance you have received is the best insurance that abundance will continue" (Koran, Sura, 14). Islam encourages you to pray to God five times a day in order to be grateful to God for His blessings.

Humble prayers to God, for all the blessings He provided us, before we go to sleep will help us to sleep well and in peace. In order to be grateful to others, we must stop being selfish and start appreciating others.

Gratitude makes us happy and peaceful. We must show our gratitude to God for giving us the sky, sun, moon, rain, relationships, food, clothing, and shelter. "Every good and perfect gift is from above, coming down from the Father of heavenly lights, who does not change like shifting shadows" (James 1:17 NIV). "When pride comes then comes the disgrace, but with humility comes wisdom" (Proverbs 11:2 NIV).

Grateful people are happier, less depressed, less stressed, and more satisfied with their lives and social relationships than those who are ungrateful. They also have more positive ways of coping with the difficulties they experience in life and are willing to seek support from other people. Grateful people sleep well, because they think positive things before they go to sleep and when they wake up. They will have less stress and more peace.

People complain about what others have not done rather than appreciating what others have done for them and the help they received from others. Gratitude is the surest way of finding God. It creates a positive life, less stress and more peace.

Our dissatisfaction and lack of happiness and peace, are primarily due to being self-absorbed and our inability to be grateful to others. We create our unhappiness by thinking about what we do not have rather than enjoying and appreciating what we have. In order to be grateful to others, we must stop being selfish and start appreciating others. The happiest people may not have the best, but they make the best of everything they have.

It is important to have true love, gratitude, and contentment to lead a happy and peaceful life. As human beings, we must practice our beliefs and grow in faith in God to strengthen our love for all others. This will reduce our stress and give us more peace beyond our imagination.

Stress and Peace in Death

Death is defined as the end of life—the irreversible stoppage of the heart, respiration, and brain activity. When we die, we leave our bodies behind, but our spirits live on. Physical death is not an end but God's plan for great joy and peace for the person making this transition.

We must realize that, we come into this world with nothing and we will leave this world with nothing. We do not know where we will be born or where we will die. God knew all about us before we were born, and it was His decision to select the places we were born and the wombs we came from. It is also His decision when and where we die.

This is emphasized many times in the Bible. "Before I formed you in the womb, I knew you before you were born, I set you apart, appointed you as a prophet to the nations" (Jeremiah 1:5 NIV).

We have assurance from God that He is always there for us. He has given us enough talents, resources, and freedom to educate ourselves and experience a good life. It is our responsibility to be dependent on Him and responsible for all our actions.

We are never completely independent but always dependent on God and His blessings. God will lead us through the plans He has laid out for our lives. We have to concentrate on making ourselves available to Him, because all of our talents and resources have been given to us by Him. He has made us the way He wants us to be. "Yet O Lord you are our father. We are the clay, you are the potter, we, are the work of your hand" (Isaiah 64:8 NIV).

God created us to be His followers and do the right thing. According to God's promise, He will direct us to do the right thing if we listen to His voice. Sometimes, we abuse our independence and try to achieve what is important to us and not what is in accordance with God's plan. We overstress the accomplishment of our desires without following God's plan. We seek our own glory and kingdom and not His. We have to understand that He will provide us with enough glory and peace if we accept Him as our companion and Savior.

We have discussed in detail the fact that we create our own stress because we work for our needs without considering what God's plans are for us. We seek peace and joy but cannot find them. We spend too much of our time on our own needs and material acquisitions.

Material things give us only temporary happiness, never permanent happiness. We always look for improvements to material things to make us happier. What we do not realize is that our happiness comes from constant companionship with God and grows from within. There is nothing wrong with using our God-given talents and acquired knowledge to produce the maximum results. We must always realize that what is given to us is not only for us, but also to help and share others in need.

The moment we use these resources for our own satisfaction, we become selfish individuals who do not care for others. We have discussed many times that everyone is given different talents and resources not only for his or her use, but also to share with others.

We will enjoy our lives and be more peaceful when we start sharing these resources with less fortunate people.

Jesus said, "I tell you the truth whatever you did for one of the least of these brothers of mine you did it for me" (Matthew 25:40 NIV).

When we start accumulating and utilizing all our resources for ourselves, then God's purpose of sharing with others is not accomplished. When God is not with us, we lose peace.

When we do not share, Jesus said, "Then they will go away to eternal punishment, but the righteous to eternal life" (Matthew 25:46 NIV).

When we do not hope for eternal life, our lives become hopeless and are without joy. When we do not have joy in our lives, we will lead miserable lives with a lot of stress and without peace.

King Solomon, son of David, King of Jerusalem, said that "Everything is meaningless" (Ecclesiastes 1:1, NIV)

> I hated all the things I toiled for under the sun, because I must leave them to one who comes after me. And who knows whether he will be a wise man or a fool. (Ecclesiastes 2:18–19 NIV).

> To the man who pleases Him God gives wisdom, knowledge and happiness, but to the sinner he gives the task of gathering and storing up wealth to hand over to the one who pleases God. (Ecclesiastes 2:26 NIV)

> I know that there is nothing better for men to be happy and does good while they live. (Ecclesiastes 3:12 NIV)

> In this meaningless life of mine I have seen both of these, a righteous man perishing in his righteousness

and the wicked man living long in his wickedness. (Ecclesiastes 7:15 NIV)

All authority in heaven and earth is given to me. Therefore go and make disciples of all nations, baptizing them in the name of the Father and Son and the Holy Spirit, and teaching them to obey everything I have commanded you. And surely I am with you always to the end of the age. (Matthew 28:18–20 NIV)

Since we do not understand death, we all fear death, and the fear does not lessen with age. The fear of death is fear of pain and suffering, the unknown, nonexistence, eternal punishment, losing control, and concern about what happens to our loved ones. Fear of death can interfere with daily life.

But God assures us, "So do not fear for I am with you; do not be dismayed for I am your God. I will strengthen you and help you. I will uphold you with my right hand" (Isaiah 41:10 NIV).

During our lives, it is very important that we live happily and joyfully. We must associate with others with affection and honesty so we all can have great lives with our families and our friends.

Most all of us worry without really understanding that worry does not help us do anything better. As a matter of fact, when we are worried and stressed, our performance will be worse than usual. We must do the best we can and stop worrying about things beyond our control.

We cannot solve all the problems in the world, but we must be kind, loving, and compassionate and help others as much as we can. We must believe that our almighty God is always there to help take care of our problems. God wants us to do our best and spread His Word to everyone. He wants us to live happily and die peacefully.

Conclusion

We all look for life to be joyful. We all want to be happy and at peace. Life is not easy and can be very complicated. The simpler we make our lives, the easier life becomes. I have mentioned numerous ways to overcome stress and obtain peace. We may never obtain complete peace, but we will feel less stressed and more at peace during our lives. It all depends on how we manage our relationships with God, family, friends and others.

When we are brought into this world, we are assured that He will take care of us. If we look at our lives, we will see that from the day we were born, during every stage of our lives, we always had people come to our assistance. During good times and bad times, God provided us with His ambassadors and angels to protect and preserve us. God is always there with us during our life journeys. When He is with us and we follow in His footsteps, our lives become more contented and peaceful.

We face ups and downs in life that we must learn to accept positively and contentedly. Life becomes more joyful, hopeful, and peaceful when we learn to love others as they are. The more we love others, the better our lives become, and love will provide us with more peace and less stress. We share our time, talents, and resources with others in need. We will start feeling good about our lives and feel more peaceful.

God created us with sufficient time, talents, and resources to lead joyful and peaceful lives. Along with this, He gave us freedom to lead the lives we want. We have been given a choice of living our own way or choosing life with Him. All around us and throughout the universe some try to live without Him.

We can try to build everything we need according to only our needs. We cannot practice true love and live our lives only for ourselves. When we live our own lives only for ourselves, we will find that the lives we live are not always full.

We begin to feel that the material things we have accumulated do not mean much. We feel lonely, stressed, and not peaceful. We feel like we are losers and could have enjoyed life more if we shared with others. We must live our lives with God and for Him. We must share our God-given time, talents, and resources with people in need. This kind of life will give us joy and peace.

Time does not wait for anyone, and we are allowed only a limited time on earth. It is essential that we live the best we can for ourselves and others. We do not know when life will end. However, we must live in happiness, peace, and hope, and when our time comes, we will leave at peace.

We must praise God in happy moments, seek God in difficult times, worship God in quiet moments, trust God in painful moments, and thank God every moment. When God is with us, we will experience His acceptance of us when we die.

> I have to realize that whatever I do has meaning only if I ask that it serves His purpose. I believe that in my present undertaking, whatever the outcome, it will be His doing. I will pray for understanding, of what it is, He would have me do. (Kengor, Paul. "God and Ronald Reagan A spiritual Life")

The Lord is my shepherd I shall not be in want. He guides me in the path of righteousness for his name sake. He makes me lie down in the green pastures, He leads me beside quiet waters He restores my soul. He guides me in the paths of righteousness for His name sake even though I walk through the valley of the shadow of death I will fear no evil. (Psalm 23:1–4 NIV)

Do not let your hearts be troubled. Trust in God, trust also in me. In my Father's house are many rooms; if it were not so, I would have told you, I am going there to prepare a place for you. I will come back and take you to be with me that you may also be where I am. You know the way to the place where I am going. (John 14:1–4 NIV)

People who live with joy, love and peace will die with joy, love and peace. Let us all trade our stressful lives for peace. God will be with all of us now and forever.

Endnotes

(1) Bill Phillips, author of *Body for Life*, was born in Golden, Colorado in 1964.

(2) Richard Carlson, PhD, 1961–2006, author and motivational speaker

(3) Dr. Martin Luther King Jr. (1929–1968), Clergyman, and leader of Civil Rights Movement

(4) Aggregate Revolving Consumer Debt Survey

(5) National Student Loan Data System for Movement (NSLDS)

(6) Information for Organization for Economic Cooperation and Development

(7) National Health and Nutrition Examination Surveys (NHANES)

(8) Federation of Red Cross and Red Crescent Societies

(9) Reported by Genocide Watch with Internal Alliance to Educate Genocides

(10) Bertrand Russell (1872–1970) was a British philosopher and antiwar activist.

(11) Mother Teresa (1910–1997) was Albanian-born and an Indian Roman Catholic by faith. She was a Nobel Prize winner.

(12) Mahatma Gandhi (1869–1948) was the leader of the Indian National Congress.

(13) Aristotle (384–322 BC) was a Greek philosopher and student of Plato.

(14) Victor Hugo (1802–1885) was a French novelist and dramatist.

(15) Albert Einstein (1879–1955) was a German physicist and wrote the theory of relativity.

(16) Oliver Wendell Homes (1809–1894) was an American physician, poet, professor, and writer.

(17) John Lennon (1940–1980) was a British-born musician and founding member of the Beatles.

(18) John F. Kennedy (1917–1963) was elected as the thirty-fifth US President in 1960.

(19) Nelson Mandela (b. 1918) was the South African President from 1994–1999.

(20) Ronald Reagan (1911–2004) was the fortieth President of the US from 1981–1989 and thirty-third Governor of California.

(21) Napoleon Bonaparte (1969–1821) was the French Emperor from 1804–1815.

(22) The Dalai Lama (b. 1935) was a spiritual leader and King of Tibet.

(23) Dr. Ronald Klatz is a physician and President of the Academy of Anti-aging.

(24) Buddha (Siddhartha Gautama, 563–483 BC) King of Magadha, India, established Buddhism in in 598 BC.

(25) *Bhagavat Gita* is a seven-hundred-word Dharmic Scripture and is a part of *Mahabharata*.

(26) John Milton (1608–1674) was English poet and freedom fighter.

(27) Hans Hugo Bruno Selye (1907–1982) was a Hungarian-born endocrinologist. He was a winner of the Nobel Prize in 1949.

(28) Natalie Goldberg (b. 1948) is an American writer and poet.

(29) *Veda* means "knowledge" and is a part of the oldest scripture of Hinduism.

(30) Plato (428–347) was a Greek philosopher.